THE MOVERS & SHAKERS OF

Medieval

~ England ~

Susannah Jowitt

A WHO'S WHO OF HISTORY'S MOST GIFTED,
FAMOUS AND INFLUENTIAL PEOPLE

ENGLISH HERITAGE

THINK
BOOKS

A Think Book for English Heritage
First published in 2006 by

Think Publishing
The Pall Mall Deposit
124-128 Barlby Road
London W10 6BL

Distributed in the United States and Canada by
Sterling Publishing Co., Inc.
387 Park Avenue South
New York, NY 10016-8810

Published in association with
English Heritage
Kemble Drive
Swindon SN2 2GZ

Author: Susannah Jowitt
Editors: Melanie Green and Emma Jones
Sub editors: Victoria Chow, Rica Dearman and Marion Thompson
Design: Lou Millward and Mark Evans
Cover design: Jes Stanfield

ISBN-10: 1-90562-407-7
ISBN-13: 978-90562-407-2

Printed and bound in Great Britain by William Clowes Ltd, Beccles, Suffolk
Cover image: Mary Evans Picture Library

With thanks to:

Thanks must go first and foremost to Dr Maurice Keen, who not only proofread the manuscript, but also agreed to write the introduction; and to Adam Harley, without whose office to escape to I would have been plagued by the infant movers and shakers in my own house. Thanks also to Emma Jones and Rica Dearman at Think Publishing, for their patience, and to all the historian friends I badgered for suggestions, especially my husband Anthony, whose memories of our Oxford history degree course were so much more accurate than my own. Finally, to Mr Burnham, wherever you are, for being a prep school history master so inspiring and memorable that, for me, the medieval era will forever be a time of colour, cacophony and utterly alive characters.

◆

Think Publishing would also like to thank:

Adele Campbell, Rob Richardson and Rene Rodgers at English Heritage, and Tania Adams, Kathi Hall, Richard Rees, Harriet Smith and Rob Turner.

Foreword

I t is a pleasure and a privilege to have been asked to contribute a brief foreword to this book by Susannah Jowitt, wife of my old friend and former pupil, Anthony Frieze. History was the subject that both he and she studied as undergraduates at Oxford, and it is on the shelves devoted to history that her book will be found in libraries and bookshops. But it is different in a distinctive way from the usual run of history books on those shelves.

Terry Jones, in his remarkable study of *Chaucer's Knight*, refers incisively in one passage to the attitude of those he calls the 'Telegraph readers' of the 14th century, and I think his metaphor may help me to explain what is different about this book. If there were natural *Telegraph* readers in those days, there must, I suppose have been natural *Guardian* readers, too, and no doubt some Top People, who if *The Times* had been available, would have taken it – for the leaders, the obituaries, and above all, for the Register with its court and social information. What Susannah has put together in her collection of brief biographical notices of 250 odd medieval 'movers and shakers' is not in any of these modes; she reports rather in the spirit in which the medieval tabloid press, if there had been such, would have put the news across, with that keen eye that tabloids have for celebrities, and for spotting and revealing the spicier and more dramatic aspects of their lives.

Professional historians like myself are on the whole readers of the quality press, and our efforts to reconstruct and interpret the past come in quality press mode, concentrating on the serious aspects of the story, and looking for themes of significance running through it. That is what the serious students of history, professional or amateur, who constitute our readership, expect of us. Susannah's book is not aimed at that audience, and no high scholarly claims are made on behalf of its racy romps through the careers of long-dead kings, bishops, barons, saints and sinners. Her book is written, not for the erudite or the would-be erudite, but for readers whose interest on history is more light-hearted, who do not want to be lumbered with in-depth historical discussions, but whose curiosity and consciousness of heritage has stirred a wish to identify the sort of people who their remote ancestors would have recognised as 'movers and shakers', and to know something of why they caught attention in their long past time. She has concentrated therefore on what found its way into the record of their individual lives on account of its news worthiness, because it was distinctive, or impressive, or scandalous, or gory, or just plain odd. This is the sort of material that puts flesh on the bones of individual identity, personalises the remembered name of a past celebrity and makes him or her still interesting now. To the highfalutin this may seem a rather tabloid approach to history; for the less grave enquirer it provides, through a gallery of pen portraits, a series of landmarks that define a serviceable way about the story of the English middle ages.

In Susannah's vignettes of her movers and shakers, their impact on their times (and subsequent history) is often assumed rather than explained. What comes across clearly is that (with the exception of Robin Hood) these were real people, the context of whose lives can be pinned down accurately in terms of dates, and of the events and circumstances of their day. She has grouped them into themed categories, according to their status and social role. Thus kings have a chapter (the first) to themselves; so do barons, bishops and great ladies; so likewise do soldiers and mercenaries, builders and master craftsmen, lawyers and administrators, rogues and rebels. A fascinating chapter gathers a diverse group at the margins of ordered society: hermits, heretics, mystics, witches and sorcerers. What all these groups have in common is that they are composed of people who were, in their different ways, celebrities and whose doings therefore were likely to be talked about, and that is why so much that remains lively and intriguing about them was remembered.

Medieval Englishmen were no less expert than their descendants in gossip and rumour-mongering, so that a certain amount of embroidery has often got into the story. Susannah's readers will be wise to remember that the memories that the past has bequeathed are not always reliably accurate. There are points of detail, including some rather arresting ones, such as the precise manner of the death of Edward II, or the precise number of bastards that Henry I recognised as his offspring, that will always remain open to question. Her readers will at the same time be grateful that she has taken care to see that whatever is eye-catching and memorable about the careers of her subjects has found a place in the pages of her book. She has made sure that they are offered some very lively reading.

Dr Maurice Keen OBE
Emeritus Fellow of Balliol
Oxford, 2006

◆

CONTENTS

CHAPTER I

◆

THE CROWNING TOUCH

Willy, Willy, Harry, Stee,
Harry, Dick, John, Harry Three;
One, two, three Neds, Richard Two,
Henries Four, Five, Six, then who?
Edwards Four, Five, Dick the Bad,
Harries twain...

The lives, loves and deaths of the medieval kings of England make modern-day soap operas look dull indeed. Madness, murder, mayhem – and the odd red-hot poker – were repeated from reign to reign; in fact, the rarities are the peaceful reigns, marked only by happy marriages and pious prosperousness.

◆

William I, king from 1066–1087   *William 'the Conqueror'*

When William stepped off his boat and fell flat on his face on an English beach in September 1066, not only was he to become the last successful invading King of England, and the one from whom we number all subsequent monarchs, but he also revealed himself as one of the earliest 'kings of spin'. As his troops gasped in horror at the bad omen of his fall, the burly Duke of Normandy rose to his feet with sand clenched in his fists and cried out: 'See, I have taken England with both my hands.' And so he had. William trounced Harold at Hastings and, despite a rather dubious claim to the throne, was crowned in Westminster Abbey within three months.

Determined, ruthless and energetic, William soon consolidated the rule of his new fiefdom and commissioned the Domesday Book (1086), an extraordinarily detailed survey of England's productive capacity, similar to a modern census, and dotted many castles, keeps and mottes (among them, the Tower of London) across England to ensure a stranglehold of security. William died at the age of 60, after falling from his horse at the Siege of Mantes, near Rouen, and was buried in Caen, Normandy. In an undignified postscript, his corpulent body would not fit in the stone sarcophagus and, after some unsuccessful prodding and jostling by the attending bishops, it burst, filling the chapel with a foul smell and dispersing the mourners.

◆

William II, king from 1087–1100   *'Rufus'*

The second William to rule England was not an admired monarch. His reign is remembered more for his viciousness, his foul-mouthed scorn for all churchmen and his long feud with the English Church. The perhaps biased summation by the monk writing the *Anglo-Saxon Chronicle* was that he was 'hated by almost all his people'.

Despite refining Anglo-Norman systems of government, which resulted in an efficiency of taxation unrivalled by anything in contemporary Europe, Rufus (so called for his red face) is more famous for his mysterious death than for anything else. In a 'whodunnit' that remains unsolved, the king was felled by an arrow while out hunting in the New Forest. Contemporary chroniclers insist it was not murder. Instead they believe that Walter Tyrell, a knight who was hunting with William, accidentally loosed an arrow and then fled, fearing he would be charged with the king's death. But Tyrell was known to be an expert archer and swore later from exile that he had not even been near the king when he was struck.

The king's body was found the next day by a group of peasants. It had been abandoned by the hunting party, including William's brother and heir, Henry, who had scarpered to protect their own interests. According to legend, a charcoal-burner called Purkis took the corpse to Winchester Cathedral.

◆

Henry I, king from 1100–1135   *'Beauclerc'*

orn in Yorkshire during his father's Harrying of the North, William the Conqueror's fourth son Henry I was the first post-Conquest monarch to be born in his own kingdom. As a result of the education that he had received as grooming for his intended 'younger son' career in the Church, Henry was also the first Norman ruler to be fluent in the English language. Despite his nickname, Henry 'Beauclerc', he was no mere scholar, but a ruler of remarkable political skill. While his brother's body was still on its way to Winchester, Henry seized power and was crowned within three days. He secured his position among Norman nobles and Anglo-Saxons alike with a show of appeasement: the Charter of Liberties, which was considered a forerunner to the Magna Carta. His marriage three months after his coronation, to Edith, daughter of King Malcolm III of Scotland, also united his Norman stock with the old line of English kings.

His marriage was a success, but he was far from faithful: Henry holds the record for the largest number of acknowledged illegitimate children born to any English king (about 25, most called 'FitzRoy', meaning 'bastard of the king'). Unfortunately, his only legitimate son, William, perished in the wreck of the *White Ship* in 1120, so when his daughter Matilda married Geoffrey of Anjou in 1127, he insisted his barons swear allegiance to her, as his heir. It was one demand too far for the English nobles and led to a long civil war after his death, known as 'the anarchy'. Henry died of food poisoning from eating 'a surfeit of lampreys' (eels) of which he was fond.

◆

Stephen, king from 1135–1154   *Stephen 'de Blois'*

tephen claimed that his uncle, King Henry I, had changed his mind on his deathbed by adopting Stephen as his heir instead of his daughter Matilda, and so persuaded the English nobles to elect him monarch instead. It was a weak claim from a man who turned out to be a weak ruler, not respected by either his subjects or his chroniclers, one of whom, Walter Map, memorably described him as 'adept at the martial arts but in other respects little more than a simpleton'.

Stephen's vacillations over alliances, his loss of control over the Church and, crucially, his failure to secure the succession to his own family, meant that by 1153 it was all over. So soft-spoken that, it was alleged, he had a stand-in to address his troops before battle, Stephen paid the price for his lack of kingly presence by having to sign a treaty promising to adopt Matilda's son, Henry Plantagenet, as his heir. He died a year later. A damning excerpt from the *Anglo-Saxon Chronicle* concludes: 'And so it lasted for 19 years while Stephen was king... the land was all undone and darkened with such deeds, and men said openly that Christ and his angels slept.'

Henry II, king from 1154–1189   *The 'lion of justice'*

Picknamed the 'lion of justice' for bringing law and order to a chaotic England, Henry II has been credited with the first written legal textbook which provided the basis for English Common Law and effectively introduced trial by jury. However, as a ruler he was seldom at home. Born in Le Mans, dying in Chinon, Henry spent two thirds of his long reign outside England.

Henry knew how to hold a grudge. His temper tantrums were legendary and led to a famous conflict with Thomas Becket, once his friend and mentor, which culminated in Becket's horrific murder. However, even this pales by comparison with the epic showdowns Henry had with his wife Eleanor of Aquitaine. So furious were their battles, they prompted the 1173–1174 Great Rebellion by his sons, who took her side. He retaliated by imprisoning her for 15 years until his death in 1189.

◆

Richard I, king from 1189–1199   *Richard 'the Lionheart'*

Just like his father before him, Richard I, as the third-born son, was never expected to ascend to the throne, yet for all the power struggles at the end of Henry II's life, Richard's accession was one of the most peaceful and unchallenged of any medieval English king. Richard knew France as his home, had sided with his mother Eleanor against his father and was more interested in military honours than in governing a large kingdom of which he knew very little. In 10 years of his reign he spent only six months in England, claiming it was 'cold and always raining'. Yet despite this, Richard the Lionheart left a greater legacy than one might have expected. His authority, even *in absentia*, was such that his English reign was never really challenged, and he created a romantic appeal so seductive that his people raised unprecedented amounts for his crusade.

To commentators, his crusading exploits confirmed him as the very acme of a prince. He conquered Cyprus on the way to the Holy Land, establishing a base for the maintenance of Christian outposts in Palestine; relieved the siege of Acre and just missed recapturing Jerusalem, all with knightly prowess, brilliant generalship and skilful diplomacy. Handsome, blond, blue-eyed and tall, Richard was the pin-up of the medieval world, lending a romance to England's image.

◆

John, king from 1199–1216   *'Soft-Sword'*

As famously favoured as Richard was, so his brother John was mythically unpopular, even down to his nicknames. While Richard was 'Coeur de Lion' or 'Lionheart', and could do no wrong, John was 'Lackland' and 'Soft-Sword', and had a reputation for treacherousness, prurient lechery and a lack of charm. His reign has been described as one of the most disastrous in English history. As one contemporary troubadour said: 'No one may ever trust him/For his heart is soft and cowardly.' At the start of his reign he lost Normandy to Philip Augustus of France; by the end, England was facing civil war and foreign invasion.

Yet John was no slouch. He was well-read, was assiduous as a judge, personally supervised the work of the exchequer, oversaw the creation of a national customs system based upon standardised weights and measures, improved the 'pipe rolls' system of accounting and helped found the English Navy. But he was beset by bad luck; in 1216, retreating from a French invasion, he lost his baggage train, including the Crown Jewels, in the marshy area known as The Wash in East Anglia. Shortly after, in October 1216, he died a broken man, some say killed by poisoned ale and others by a surfeit of peaches. Rarely has an English ruler been so vilified. Matthew Paris, the monk and contemporary chronicler, trenchantly summed up his view of John's reign: 'Foul as it is... Hell itself is defiled by the fouler presence of King John.' In 2005, the BBC's *History* magazine selected him as the 13th century's worst Briton.

◆

Henry III, king from 1216–1272   *'Henry of Winchester'*

enry III, aged nine, was hastily crowned in Gloucester on his father's death in 1216. One of England's more opaque medieval monarchs, Henry was also the longest-reigning ruler between 1066 and 1485, and the only monarch until the late 14th century to be educated rigorously as a ruler. Once he had taken up the reins of the monarchy it quickly became clear that he was no pushover. Pious, obsessed with the cult of the Anglo-Saxon saint King Edward the Confessor and austere in his dress and habits, Henry was keen to restore royal authority and the majesty of his office. He looked to France, his Lusignan half-brothers and his French in-laws for the autocratic model of kingship.

Initially criticised by his subjects for advancing foreign favourites, it was one of his former favourites, Simon de Montfort, who proved to be a thorn in Henry's side in the 1250s and 1260s. De Montfort led disgruntled barons into civil war against the king, forcing Henry to abandon his wild dream of winning the crown of Sicily for his second son, Edmund. The tide of war ebbed and flowed, but finally turned in favour of Henry and his eldest son, Edward 'Longshanks', when the barons began to suspect that De Montfort had gone too far with his reforming zeal. After the bloody battle of Evesham in 1265, control was effectively handed over to its victor, Prince Edward, who imposed stern terms on the rebels in return for admission to his peace.

When Henry died in November 1272 he was laid to rest in the rebuilt Westminster Abbey.

◆

Edward I, king from 1272–1307   *Edward 'Longshanks'*

Known as Lord Edward during his glory days on St Louis's last crusade of 1270, Edward 'Longshanks' (so-called because of his long-legged six-foot two-inch frame) came to the throne on a wave of military prowess, having earned his spurs both at home and abroad. Even though his crusading was not very effective, Edward I tapped into the English love of valour and was hailed by contemporary chroniclers as the second Lionheart, famous for warding off a would-be assassin by bludgeoning him with a metal stool.

Building on his military experiences in the crusades, Edward wasted no time in conquering Wales, forcing it into submission by 1284 and commencing construction of a string of massive stone castles encircling the principality, as at Caernarvon. He then turned his attentions to Scotland, first by trying to influence the succession and then by force, razing Berwick-upon-Tweed. He then raced up beyond Edinburgh and removed the symbol of Scottish nationalism, the Stone of Destiny, from Scone Palace. He then moved it to King Edward's Chair in Westminster (on which all future kings and queens were crowned), where it remained until 1996. Opposition, led by characters such as William 'Braveheart' Wallace and Robert the Bruce, stymied Edward's ambitions, but not before he'd earned his nickname 'The Hammer of the Scots'.

Edward was married twice. His first wife, Eleanor of Castile, bore him 16 children and left him bereft on her death in 1290. Nine years later, at the rather advanced age of 60, he married Marguerite of France, with whom he had three more children. When he died, he was on his way to fight yet another campaign against the Scots, despite his great age of 68.

◆

Edward II, king from 1307–1327   *The first Prince of Wales*

Edward II's reign started full of promise. The first English prince to hold the title of Prince of Wales, Edward was as physically impressive as his father, who had trained him from childhood in the arts of warfare and statecraft. But he lacked the fire in his belly so necessary for medieval monarchs, preferring extravagant entertainments to anything useful or businesslike.

Edward neglected his wife, Isabella of France, and, indeed, most of the court, preferring to spend time with his friends plotting how to defraud his barons and councillors of their powers. In 1307, one such friend, Piers Gaveston, was banished by Edward I for being an unsuitable influence on his son; Edward II's very first act as monarch later that year was to recall him, giving him the (hitherto royal) earldom of Cornwall and the hand of his own niece. The outraged barons twice insisted on Gaveston's banishment, but each time Edward ensured his return. Finally, in 1312, the barons went to war, assassinated Gaveston and forced Edward to rule under a baronial committee (essentially, a parliament of lords). His later favourite, Hugh le Despenser the Younger, caused similar problems, but this time Edward and the Despensers won, ruling England for the next five years.

But Edward's disasters were not confined to the domestic front. His defeat at the hands of Robert Bruce at Bannockburn resulted in the almost total collapse of his power in Scotland and heralded the beginning of the end for his reign. Routed in September, captured in October, deposed in January in favour of his son Edward III, he was dead by the following October. According to the traditional story, as Sir Thomas More later described it: 'The King was suddenly seized and, while a great mattress... suffocated him, a plumber's iron, heated intensely hot, was introduced through a tube into his secret parts so that it burned the inner portions beyond the intestines.'

◆

Edward III, king from 1327–1377   *'King of France'*

E dward III was one of the most successful medieval kings, with an unchallenged 50-year reign marked by the expansion of English territory through wars in Scotland and France, and a happy marriage which produced five healthy sons. But Edward certainly had his own struggles at the beginning. Crowned at 14 when his father was still alive, he was initially the puppet of his powerful mother, Isabella of France, and her consort Roger Mortimer. He married at 15 and was in power at 18 when he overthrew and executed Mortimer and sidelined his mother. Once the domestic dust had settled Edward launched the Hundred Years' War with a claim, through his mother, to the throne of France. With his eldest son, the 'Black Prince', by his side, Edward notched up some epic victories at Crécy and Poitiers. Despite the cycle of gain and reversal in the ensuing generations of war, English kings would continue to claim the title 'King of France' for hundreds of years afterwards.

◆

Richard II, king from 1377–1399   *An 'unkingly' king*

Richard II took to the throne at the tender age of 10. He had been born at Epiphany, giving rise to the legend that he was destined for great things. Indeed, it looked promising at first. Four years into his reign, he single-handedly defused the Peasants' Revolt of 1381 through courage, youthful disingenuousness and a crafty pardon for Wat Tyler, the revolt's charismatic leader. But as he grew up, Richard faltered, showing a striking inability to handle the essential wheeling and dealing of 14th-century politics and diplomacy and, more crucially, failing to produce an heir from two marriages.

Yet again, it was the sidelining of his nobles in blatant favour of a chosen few loved ones – Robert de Vere in particular – that provoked real animosity and distrust towards the king. In protest at the king's vacillations in France (he preferred peace, where many lords preferred the profits of war) some particularly disaffected barons formed themselves into a gang called the

Lords Appellant and challenged the king. The resulting skirmishes saw the king in the Tower of London and the execution or exile of most of his cronies.

For the next decade Richard ruled even more meekly, preferring the dashing bravado of tournaments over the messy realities of war. But this only set him back further. His Scottish campaign was indecisive, the 28-year treaty with France was scorned as the act of a coward and even his sensible policies in Ireland were seen as 'unkingly'. Yet Richard saw himself as the very embodiment of 'God's own prince' and embarked on a purge in 1397. He exiled or executed the Lords Appellant, tried to avert a succession crisis by exiling one contender – his cousin and childhood playmate, Henry Bolingbroke – and generally alienated even hitherto neutral subjects with his autocratic ways. However, things didn't go as planned. Initially fighting merely to have his massive inheritance returned, Bolingbroke ultimately usurped the king's reign and himself ruled as king for 14 years, from 1399 to 1413, while Richard was left to die in Pontefract Castle.

◆

Henry V, king from 1413–1422   *'Prince Hal'*

From the outset, the young King Henry V made it clear that he wanted to govern England as the secure ruler of a united nation, and that past differences were to be forgotten. He was a devout church-goer, gave freely to the poor and even reinstated the estates of old enemies. Backed by a united nobility and even by the commons of his parliament, Henry could now concentrate on foreign affairs – and the hitherto suspended war with France. His superb victory on the field at Agincourt in 1415 was merely the first step. He took command of the English Channel and launched a military campaign that brought the English armies to the very walls of Paris. By 1420, he was heir and regent of France, married to the French king's daughter, Catherine, and at the height of his powers. Then disaster struck – he died of dysentery aged only 35 – and the momentum of his advances was soon lost.

◆

Henry VI, king from 1422–1461 and 1470–1471   *Henry of Windsor*

y the time Henry VI began to rule England, he had already become both disenchanted with war and disdainful of dynastic attachments. He had inherited the throne at the age of nine and was subjected to a 15-year regency characterised by infighting among his uncles and prolonged campaigns against France. When he came of age in 1437, Henry proved to be a profoundly pious man. Although he was a keen patron of arts and education, he lacked the iron spine and worldly wisdom necessary to rule effectively. Nobles soon split into pro-war and pro-peace factions: Henry sided with the pro-peace (Lancastrian) Beauforts, alienating the pro-war House of York.

After marrying Margaret of Anjou, Henry ceded Anjou and Maine to France, a hugely unpopular move. After the disastrous loss of Gascony in 1453, Henry had a mental breakdown, precipitating a power struggle between Queen Margaret and Richard, Duke of York. York emerged victorious and was appointed Protector of the Realm in 1454, and soon after the country fell into the chaos of the Wars of the Roses. In 1461, after enduring crushing defeats, Henry effectively lost his throne to Edward IV. Four years later, he was captured by the Yorkists and imprisoned in the Tower of London. He was briefly restored to the throne by his wife and his old enemy, Richard Neville, Earl of Warwick (known as 'the Kingmaker'). But Henry lost his throne again after the Yorkist victory at Tewkesbury, which also saw the death of his son, the Prince of Wales. He died in the Tower of London in May 1471, probably murdered.

◆

Edward IV, king from 1461–1470 and 1471–1483 *The first York king*

ngland's first Yorkist monarch, Edward IV inherited the struggle for power from his father, Richard, Duke of York. He based his claim to the throne on their descent from Lionel of Antwerp through the Mortimer line and on the illegitimacy of the Lancastrian line (going back to Henry IV's resumption of the throne some 50 years before). Hastily crowned by a pro-York faction in London, it wasn't until the decisive Battle of Towton in 1461 that Edward could feel in any way secure on his throne. His rule was largely untroubled until 1469 when he was dethroned and forced to flee to the continent. He was restored to the throne in 1471 and ruled thereafter in peace.

◆

Richard III, king from 1483–1485   *'Honest Diccon'*

he last English monarch to die in battle, Richard III is one of our most famous villains, memorably brought to life first by Thomas More and then by William Shakespeare, who depicted him as a hunchbacked grotesque with a withered arm, who hacked and murdered his way to the English throne. The truth, needless to say, isn't quite so crystal clear.

It is likely that Richard used any means available to secure his hold on the throne; however, as 'Honest Diccon', he was known to be a fair, just and generous governor of the North, making large grants to the Church and always staying true to his brother, Edward IV. Certainly, he was initially supported by the bulk of the nobility. His coronation in 1483 – that of the last Plantagenet king – was attended by almost the entire peerage.

In what could be seen as admirably resolute kingship in a time of anarchy, he had ruthlessly removed the challenge to his throne by his nephews, the two young sons of Edward IV and Elizabeth Woodville. First he had them declared illegitimate by the Act of Parliament known as *Titulus Regius*, then he had them locked up in the Tower of London, where – it is thought – they were subsequently murdered. However, he allowed too many enemies to rally to the standard of the nearest possible heir, Henry Tudor, which led to the battle of Bosworth in 1485 and, ultimately, the end of the medieval age.

CHAPTER II

◆

ROYAL FAVOURITES & MISTRESSES

Rosamund Clifford, c. 1140–1176   *Henry II's mistress*

Famous in English folklore for her gentle beauty, 'fair Rosamund' was the favoured mistress of Henry II in his later years, kept secret from his fiery queen, Eleanor of Aquitaine. Romantic history holds that, having met her while staying at her father's castle during his Welsh campaigns, Henry built a love nest for her deep in the forest at Woodstock.

Although she died relatively young – in her early 30s – the more colourful stories that a furiously jealous Queen Eleanor had Clifford poisoned are Elizabethan inventions. Two decades after her death the Bishop of Lincoln visited the nunnery at Godstow where Clifford died and noticed her tomb was being venerated as a shrine, laden with flowers and candles. Calling Clifford a 'harlot', the Bishop threw her remains and tomb out of the church, but local people still prayed at her new tomb in the cemetery until it was destroyed during the dissolution of the monasteries nearly 350 years later.

◆

Hodierna, born c. 1145   *Richard I's surrogate mother*

Proof that a woman didn't need to sleep with a king to profit from his favouritism, Hodierna was Richard I's wet-nurse. Such was Richard's love for his substitute mother that he settled estates on her, including one that was then named after her, Knoyle Hodierne, in Wiltshire.

He elevated her socially to the point where her own son was able to become Abbot of Cirencester and a celebrated scholar. Intriguingly this son, known as Alexander Neckham, has also been recorded as

Alexander Nequam, meaning 'bad', from his reputation as a sorcerer and necromancer – allegedly conjuring up the dead to elicit information about the future.

◆

Piers Gaveston, 1284–1312   *Favourite of Edward II*

Infamous as much for his relationship with Edward II as for the hatred he incited among the English nobles, Piers Gaveston alienated the English court with his foreign ways. In fact 'Brother Perrot', as he was called by Edward, was among the less corrupt of the royal favourites in this period, staying loyal to Edward until his murder. In return, Edward made him the Earl of Cornwall.

By all accounts Gaveston was handsome, witty, charming and athletic. He made some of his enemies through his skill at the knightly arts, such as when he defeated the king's cousin, Thomas Lancaster, in a jousting tournament.

At Edward's coronation Gaveston openly flaunted his preferred status by strutting about in imperial purple – when even the highest-born nobles wore mere cloth of gold – and scorned his less-favoured peers with breathtaking arrogance. Unsurprisingly, Gaveston had a knack for making enemies – most fatefully Edward's bride, Queen Isabella, who engineered his exile in 1312.

He returned illegally that same year and was captured and beheaded by his rivals. Edward remained generous to Gaveston's memory, paying both his daughter and widow a huge allowance and taking them and many of their servants into the royal household.

Hugh le Despenser the Younger, 1286–1326 *Favourite of Edward II*

reedy, rash and ruthless, Edward II's other fabulously unpopular favourite, Hugh le Despenser the Younger, started on his path to infamy with a couple of lucky breaks. He effectively bought his wife Eleanor Clare, granddaughter of Edward I, by wiping out her other grandfather's debts. Soon after her forced marriage Eleanor unexpectedly became one of the three heiresses of the late Earl of Gloucester. This turned Le Despenser from a minor baronial heir into one of England's wealthiest magnates in one stroke. His preference for force over persuasion served him well over the next few years. Not only did this prove useful at court, but also at home, where his hunger for power and wealth knew no barriers.

Still in his 20s, Le Despenser unlawfully seized Tonbridge Castle in 1315, broke the rules of custody by murdering a Welsh hostage in his care in 1316 and wrested estates and lands from his rivals. His tyranny and ruthlessness were running rampant.

He was briefly exiled in 1321, but restored to favour within the year. Five years later, when Edward II was deposed, Le Despenser finally met his end. He was hung, drawn and quartered, then beheaded. His head was stuck on the gates of London like any common or garden traitor.

◆

William de la Pole, 1396–1450   *Earl, Marquis and Duke of Suffolk*

epresenting the zenith of the De la Pole family's power, William de la Pole also proved its undoing. In his early years he was renowned for being the very embodiment of chivalry. By the end, however, he had been transformed into the hated favourite of Henry VI, enjoying the profits of extortion and seen to be guilty of perverting justice at every turn.

Vigorous war campaigning initially drew the attention of Henry V, who promoted him into high positions of command, but it was not military might alone that lifted De la Pole so high. Through an advantageous marriage, De la Pole became allied to the Beaufort faction, which dominated the rule of the young King Henry VI. But in a few short years it had all gone wrong. De la Pole's unpopular policies, his control over the king and his rapacious profiteering left him exposed and his rivals' jealousy came to a head in 1450. Although the king fought off De la Pole's execution after his impeachment for 'sundry treasons and misprisions', he was forced to send him into exile.

While seeking to cross the English Channel De la Pole was overtaken by a 'great ship', seized and brought on board. When told the name of the ship was *Nicholas of the Tower*, De la Pole knew his end had come. Years before, the astrologer Stacey had told De la Pole that he would 'die a shameful death' and had warned him 'to beware of the Tower'. Sure enough, once on board the ship, his head was brutally struck off with a rusty sword by 'one of the lewdest of the ship's company'. Ruin for the family, however, was not immediate. Henry VI restored all confiscated estates to De la Pole's widow, Alice, and a century later his descendant, Cardinal Pole, was a prominent servant to Queen Mary.

◆

Alice Perrers, d. 1400   *Edward III's mistress*

Whether witch or mere wanton, Alice Perrers brought some colour to the dying years of Edward III's reign. After a long and faithful marriage to his wife Philippa, in whose service the humbly born Perrers was employed, the ageing widowed king was, it was alleged, at the 'Good Parliament' of 1376, inveigled into a relationship with the married Perrers by means of witchcraft.

A Dominican friar was said to have fashioned two pictures of Edward and Perrers which, when suffused with the incense of strange herbs and plants picked under a full moon, caused the king to fixate upon this young woman. For the last 10 years of Edward's life, Perrers received gifts of land and jewels and grew in power at court.

Not content, Perrers interfered in the proceedings of the courts of law to secure sentences in favour of her friends and those who had paid for her favour. This led the Good Parliament to forbid all women from practising in the law courts and to force Perrers into exile, where she stayed until the last year of Edward's life.

◆

Sir Richard Ratcliffe, 1430–1485   *Richard III's henchman*

Richard 'the Rat' Ratcliffe was friends with Richard III while the latter was still Duke of Gloucester. Ratcliffe grew in power thanks to his valiant battle performances. By the 1470s, he had been knighted on the field at Tewkesbury, had been granted land and become constable of Barnard Castle, and was a member of Richard III's inner council at Middleham.

After the failed Lancastrian rebellion of 1483, Ratcliffe was rewarded for faithful service with numerous grants and forfeited estates, giving him an income larger than most barons. Two years later, he was killed fighting alongside Richard III and William Catesby at Bosworth.

William Catesby, 1440–1485   *Richard III's henchman*

William 'the Cat' Catesby was a self-made lawyer from Northamptonshire who had astutely manoeuvred himself into powerful positions with up-and-coming Yorkists such as Lord Zouche, Lord Scrope and the Duke of Buckingham, gaining a reputation for extortion and chicanery along the way.

In 1484, his skill at combining his 'management expertise' with political intrigue peaked when he was made speaker of the commons – only to fall again, this time literally, when he was executed after the battle of Bosworth.

◆

Viscount Francis Lovell, 1454–c. 1487   *Richard III's henchman*

Unlike William Catesby and Richard Ratcliffe, Viscount Francis Lovell was no arriviste, but an old-fashioned medieval hero. Among his tenants, he was looked upon as being of almost equal importance to the monarch; his word was law, his favour was courted and his anger feared. He was heir to a vast inheritance, related to some of the great nobles of the age, both Lancastrian and Yorkist, and grew up with Richard, Duke of Gloucester, in the great castle of Middleham. There, the two boys were taught chivalric behaviour and aristocratic skills, from Latin and law to dancing and music.

When Gloucester became King Richard III in 1483, Lovell carried the third sword at his coronation. Later that year, the childhood friend had been elevated with the granting of various estates and titles, including Lord Chamberlain of the King's Household, to one of the most powerful men in England. Unlike 'the Cat' and 'the Rat', Lovell managed to escape Bosworth. Later, he nearly captured Henry VII in a revolt in Yorkshire but, instead, was forced to flee again. This time he went to Ireland.

Still resolute in the cause of the House of York, Lovell came back to fight against Henry VII once more, supporting the pretender Lambert Simnel at the battle of Stoke in June 1487. He was last seen fighting furiously in the heat of the battle, then swimming across the River Trent with his horse and scrambling up the opposite bank. Under cover of darkness he fled to his house near Oxford and, not daring to trust even his servants, he incarcerated himself in a secret underground chamber, presumably wishing to remain hidden until he could find some means of escape from the country. What happened next is an intriguing mystery. It would appear that Lovell was then unable to open the door of his chamber and, having told no one he was there, died of suffocation.

Over 200 years later, in 1708, workmen discovered the chamber. When they broke in they found a skeleton sitting at a table, the hand resting on a bundle of papers. Had Lovell written his side of the story? We'll never know for sure. As the air rushed into the long-sealed nook, both the bony hand and the papers crumbled away to dust.

◆

THE PIOUS: ARCHBISHOPS, CARDINALS, MONKS, HOLY MEN & ONE POPE

Lanfranc, 1005–1089   *Archbishop of Canterbury*

As the first post-conquest Archbishop of Canterbury, Lanfranc has gone down in history as the man who obtained the pope's sanction of William I's invasion of England and thus conferred the appearance of a holy war on an opportunistic act of aggression. The defending King Harold was thereby deemed a usurper and an oath-breaker and his defeat at Hastings was lent an air of righteousness by papal support.

Lanfranc went on to mould Anglo-Norman ecclesiastical policy by replacing nearly all Saxon bishops and abbots with Normans, separating civil and church courts and holding regular synods. He went on to espouse the cause of the English Church, loyally uphold the primacy of his own see of Canterbury above that of York (with what, some historians say, were forged documents), help reform the Church in Scotland, enforce the observance of celibacy among the clergy, rebuild Canterbury Cathedral, found hospitals for the sick and indigent and give to widows and the poor.

As William's occasional regent, Lanfranc even bore arms for his ruler. He repressed a revolt in William's absence in 1074, and showed energy and pragmatic wisdom in dealing with affairs of state.

◆

St Anselm, 1033–1109   *Archbishop of Canterbury*

Described as 'the model of all ecclesiastical perfection' and, from childhood, loved by all who knew him, St Anselm stands out from both laymen and clergymen of his time as being a reluctant careerist. He never really wanted the limelight or adulation of his peers, yet still managed to reach the very pinnacle of the English Church, becoming the Archbishop of Canterbury.

Born in the mountains of Italy, educated in the rolling hills of Normandy and brought to prominence in England, Anselm's intellectual and spiritual gifts marked him out for success from the start. Yet as a young lad, Anselm questioned his entry into monasticism, wondering whether he'd be better off using his inheritance to relieve the needy. However, after only three years as a simple monk he was elected as the prior of the Abbey of Bec, aged only 30.

Already bemoaning the time spent away from his writings, he was asked to be abbot in 1078. His biographer, Eadmer, records a strange scene: Anselm falling prostrate before the brethren and begging them tearfully not to lay this burden on him; whereupon the monks in turn fell at his feet and beseeched him with just as many tears to take the post, which he did.

Anselm was just as reluctant 15 years later, when a bed-ridden William II finally dealt with the vacant post of Archbishop of Canterbury and named him as the successor. He refused the honour, but was dragged by force to the king's bedside, where a pastoral staff was thrust into his reluctant hand. He was then pushed up to the altar, where a 'Te Deum' was sung in celebration. But Anselm's trials were just beginning, what with William Rufus's thuggery, feuding between Church leaders and his exile only four years after being enthroned. Even when William was killed and Henry I invited Anselm back, the new ruler was just as intent on maintaining a royal grip on the Church; Anselm found himself back in exile in 1103, dying only two years after his return, in 1109.

Anselm's real contribution to history, however, lies with his writings. During almost 50 years of rigorous examination, he produced works which covered the whole of Catholic doctrine, from the conundrum of the Holy Spirit to questions of predestination and free will.

Gilbert of Sempringham, 1083–1189 *Founder of the Gilbertine Order*

Steered away from a military or knightly career because he was deemed ill-favoured by his wealthy Norman father, Gilbert of Sempringham was the only Englishman ever to found a monastic order which housed religious men and women together. It produced a chain of 26 convents, monasteries and missions under the auspices of the Gilbertine Order (later suppressed under Henry VIII). Gilbert was canonized only 12 years after his death.

Exiled to Paris by a disappointed father, Sempringham became a teacher and then, on his return to England, a clerk in the Bishop of Lincoln's household. He seems to have held non-monastic kind of church life in disdain, being only reluctantly ordained as a deacon when he was in his 40s and refusing the Archdeaconry of Lincoln, saying that he knew no surer way to perdition.

In 1131, with his father now dead, Sempringham returned to his birthplace of Sempringham, immediately using his inheritance to found what was later known as the Gilbertine Order and to start construction of his first convent. Thereafter, his life is marked by extraordinary austerity and single-mindedness regarding the governance of his order, occasionally rudely interrupted by the corruptions of the outside world.

In 1165, when he was already in his 80s, he was summoned before Henry II's Justices at Westminster to answer charges of having helped Thomas Becket in exile; five years later some of his lay-brothers rose up against him and spread serious rumours of sexual malpractice. Sempringham didn't let his age stand in the way of a spirited self-defence, however.

This time, King Henry stood up for him and the pope eventually cleared him of all suspicion. Only when troubled by the infirmities of old age and blindness did Sempringham hand over the reigns of the order. He lived to be over 100 years of age.

Nicholas Brakspear, 1100–1159 *English pope*

Remarkably little is known about the early life of Pope Adrian IV, the only English pope. All we know from the *Chronicles of St Albans* is that when the young Nicholas Brakspear applied to the monastery to be a monk, the abbot there found him somehow deficient. He said to him: 'Have patience, my son, and stay at school yet a while till you are better fitted for the position you desire.' In the event, he did not follow this advice, instead going off to France and rising to be abbot of a monastery near Arles.

His reforming zeal led to the lodging of complaints against him by French clergymen, but this just brought him to the attention of the pope. After a successful spell laying down papal law in Scandinavia, Brakspear was elected Pope Adrian IV in 1154. But his was not an easy ride. Banditry, disorder and the murder of a cardinal led to the previously unheard-of step of the pope placing an interdict on Rome.

More significant for the English was the Donation of Ireland, whereby Adrian, in dealings with chronicler John of Salisbury, gave and granted Hibernia to Henry II to hold by hereditary right. Henry, then just 22, already had his hands full enough with restive barons, stirring Welshmen and brewing trouble in his French dominions to mount a military campaign into Ireland and so the donation remained, for the moment, just a gesture.

Adrian himself seemed to doubt his own achievements, telling Salisbury that the office of pope was 'a thorny one, beset on all sides by sharp pricks', and that he wished he had never left England or had, at least, lived out life in his Provencal monastery, but that he had 'not dared to refuse the Lord's bidding'.

He died in 1159, on the brink of excommunicating his former ally, Emperor Frederick Barbarossa.

Thomas Becket, 1120–1170 *English saint*

Probably the most famous Englishman of the Middle Ages – and among the most controversial – Thomas Becket's grisly death, his canonization and the cult of pilgrimage that immediately sprang up around him, make his actual life look all the more a study of contrasts. Tall and handsome, with a beaky nose and bright eyes, his personality always invited friendship and charmed those who met him. But he was never revered as a scholar and, even when life went well for him, he showed signs of being highly strung. He suffered from stress-related ailments and was reported to have had a slight stammer.

Rather prosaically, he started life as a London merchant's son and worked as an accountant to a London banker before joining the household of Archbishop Theobald of Canterbury. By the time he became chancellor to Henry II, Becket – although not yet in full orders as a monk – had carved out a niche as being worldly, diplomatic, charming and prone to blowing his riches on a magnificent lifestyle. On an embassy to Paris in 1158, he took with him 250 servants, eight large wagons laden with furnishings and plate, and 24 changes of clothes.

Soon inseparable from the king, Becket took up arms on his behalf, actually fighting in full armour on French campaigns and even defeating respected knights at jousting tournaments. Henry II must have thought that appointing such a worldly friend to the post of Archbishop of Canterbury would keep the sometimes troublesome Church (and papacy) off his back. Imagine his shock when Becket seemed to transform from pleasure-loving chancellor to ascetic champion of the Church, almost immediately taking up the cudgels and challenging Henry on matters of ecclesiastical jurisdiction and immunity from the Crown.

Yet this change wasn't quite so dramatic if looked at from another angle. When he had been chancellor, Becket had aggressively fought for royal rights and status and, as Archbishop of Canterbury, he argued with the same vigour for the protection of all Church rights. By 1163, the king and Becket had dramatically fallen out. By 1164, Becket – who had fought Henry for clerical immunity from secular trials – found himself on trial. Ignoring the legal and physical threats – undeterred that he had alienated many of his colleagues with his high-handedness and playing up to the crowd by actually carrying his own cross into the trial – Becket denied the jurisdiction of the royal court and fled, in disguise, into exile abroad.

His six-year exile turned an almost personal conflict between him and Henry into an international *cause célèbre*, the flames of which were fanned by a relentless propaganda campaign waged by Becket. In 1165 he dramatically converted to an ascetic way of life, wearing a hair shirt and flagellating himself violently and publicly.

When Henry overplayed his hand by having the Archbishop of York crown his young son as Henry III, Becket was able to return, but their dispute was still an open wound. Almost immediately Becket was back to his high-handed ways, refusing to lift his excommunication of the priests involved in young Henry's coronation. Suddenly, what had been a royal sulk flared up into a temper tantrum. King Henry II, in Normandy for Christmas and possibly feeling the excesses of the season, is said to have shouted out the famous words: 'Will nobody rid me of this turbulent priest?'

Four knights took him at his word and raced to England, and to Canterbury. It is probable that they came to their senses on the crossing and were merely going to arrest Becket. Once they were at Canterbury Cathedral, however, Becket's calm, uncompromising refusal to go with them caused tempers to flare and events slid out of control. In the ensuing fracas, one of Becket's entourage had his arm cut to the bone trying to protect his master; Becket himself was cut down and butchered in the north transept of his own church. The brutal manner of his murder ensured that Becket became the most famous martyr in English history.

Within a matter of days the miracles at his tomb began – 703 were recorded within a decade – and the cult of pilgrimage was sustained even into the Reformation by the sale of Canterbury Water, supposedly an inexhaustible supply of Becket's diluted blood. In life, Becket was one of the least successful and least supported archbishops in English history, but in death, the issues for which he fought were resolved and his legacy as both saint and martyr put him at the forefront of the medieval age. In 1174, four years after his former friend's death, Henry II performed a very public penance at Becket's tomb. It was clear even then who would be remembered longer.

◆

Stephen Langton, 1165–1228 *Archbishop of Canterbury*

enowned as the man who broke the hold of the papacy on the English Crown, and set the wheels in motion for the Magna Carta by his insistence that King John uphold the liberties granted by Henry I (an oath which John promptly broke), Stephen Langton was born into relative obscurity in Lincolnshire. A great example of how a man could rise from humble gentility to the very pinnacles of success and fame in the Middle Ages, he was regarded at one point as the most learned man in Christendom and the foremost English churchman of his era.

From the start of his accepted tenure as Archbishop of Canterbury, Langton had two objectives: in the short term, to restrain King John's lawlessness and mediate between him and his aggrieved barons and, in the long term, to direct his energies towards creating and preserving the political and ecclesiastical independence of England. Both aims were achieved with the signing of the Magna Carta. There was a blip, however.

A sulky King John won the ear of the pope and Langton was suspended
– even, absurdly, excommunicated by Pope Innocent – until the deaths of
both king and pope in 1216, whereupon Langton was reinstated.

Throughout all this, Langton was remarkable in his sagacity, humility
and steely nerve, and revealed a clever ability to play to the crowd. A perfect
example of this is when he presided over one of the most splendid ceremonies
ever performed in England: the 'translation' of the relics of St Thomas Becket
in Canterbury Cathedral. Langton will go down in ecclesiastical history as the
man who, with his 'Constitutions of Stephen Langton' at the Council of Osney
in April 1222, set down the earliest provincial Church canons, still regarded
as binding in English Church courts, and inadvertently paved the way for the
final break with Rome under Henry VIII 300 years later.

◆

St Simon Stock, 1165–1265   *English Carmelite*

According to Carmelite traditions, St Simon Stock was the English
Carmelite to whom the order's famous 'brown scapular' (two small
squares of cloth or paper bearing religious images, joined by two bands of
cloth tethering it round the body under the clothes) was given by a vision of
the Virgin Mary with the words: 'This shall be the privilege for you and for
all the Carmelites, that anyone dying in this habit shall be saved.'

Certainly, the Carmelites flourished under his generalship. Even though he
was over 80 years of age when elected, he founded houses in the university
towns of Cambridge, Oxford, Paris and Bologna, spread the order widely
across southern and western Europe – and throughout England – and revised
the rules of the order to make them mendicant friars rather than hermits.

Legend says that he began his pious existence as a hermit himself, living from the age of 12 in a tree trunk ('stock' being derived from the Old English for 'tree trunk') and later becoming an itinerant preacher in the Holy Land, before retreating in the face of advancing Muslims.

◆

Pandulph, d. 1226 *Papal envoy*

Despite his unpromising position as a Roman-born papal envoy, Pandulph was pivotal in saving England from a French invasion in 1213, was noted in the Magna Carta as one of those by whose counsel the Charter was influenced, and even ended up virtually ruling the country during Henry III's minority.

These events could not have been predicted from his disastrous start in trying to persuade King John to back down from the argument over the Archbishopric of Canterbury that had led to a five-year interdict. Pandulph was sent packing from their first meeting, with John's threats to hang him if he came to England again still ringing in his ears. Two years later, in 1213, he fared better. With the threat of a French invasion hanging over him, the king submitted to the pope's choice of Stephen Langton as archbishop and, in a historic moment, John surrendered the Crown of England to become a fiefdom of the pope. Pandulph then called off the French dogs. Continuing to go to and fro between Rome and England, Pandulph was nominally on John's side during the Magna Carta negotiations and was quick to execute the papal bull which excommunicated the barons who would not obey Pope Innocent's annulment of the Charter. This stood him in good stead in 1218, when he was sent as a proper papal legate to enforce the Holy See's suzerainty over the throne. With the barons in a muddle, Pandulph was able to assume the regency from 1219–1221. It was a successful administration; the country's revenue was increased, justice was firmly administered and beneficial treaties with France were signed. But it ended abruptly when he came up against Stephen Langton who managed to break the papacy's grip. Pandulph resigned in July 1221.

◆

Boniface of Savoy, 1217–1270   *Archbishop of Canterbury*

pparently one of the least spiritual Archbishops of Canterbury, Boniface of Savoy was largely hated by the English for being foreign-born. Nevertheless, he was a marvellously pragmatic prelate who not only managed to pay off a huge Episcopal debt of 22,000 marks, but also built and endowed a great hospital at Maidstone and, under papal instruction, finished the Great Hall at the Palace of Lambeth. Nominated in 1241 to the see of Canterbury by his niece Queen Eleanor (wife of Henry III), Savoy's tenure did not start particularly well. He visited Canterbury once in 1244, but only when the dust of various papal successions had settled in 1249 – a full eight years after his appointment – was enthroned there with the greatest pomp at Canterbury.

With an overbearing manner that just compounded the English view of foreign clergy, Savoy soon proposed draconian economies, with a series of ever-more dramatic visitations to the dioceses. In London he met with unexpected resistance at the Priory of St Bartholomew (now more famous as St Bart's Hospital) from the sub-prior and his brethren, who pointed out politely that they recognised the authority of the Bishop of London before an outsider from Canterbury. Savoy was so incensed that he knocked the sub-prior to the ground, whereupon the outraged Londoners fell upon him, tearing his vestments and revealing the chain mail he wore underneath. Rescued by his bodyguard, Savoy escaped across the river to Lambeth, where he holed up and promptly excommunicated the Bishop of London and all the brothers of St Bartholomew's.

He defended his actions to a papal court and a compromise was reached between Savoy and his clergy after the turmoil of the Barons' War, during which he initially seemed to side with the barons before drifting over to the king. Savoy returned to England in 1265 with a triumphant monarch and headed the Church in relative peace and quiet until 1269. Intending to accompany the then Lord Edward on crusade in 1270, Savoy died en route in his home country.

◆

Thomas Cantelupe, 1218–1282   *St Thomas of Hereford*

Born into an influential family, Thomas Cantelupe seemed destined for a distinguished academic career, but the turbulent times in which he lived pushed him to political prominence. Supporting the popular side during the Barons' War of the 1260s, Cantelupe was appointed their advocate before St Louis at the Council of Amiens. His success there suddenly made him the natural choice to be Chancellor of England following Henry III's defeat at the Battle of Lewes.

During his stint, he was an adept administrator renowned for his judicial wisdom and fairness. On the death of Simon de Montfort, he fled into exile, but was allowed back in 1272. Already known to be a particularly holy and charitable priest, he was rewarded with the Bishopric of Hereford. When travelling in his diocese, he would ask every child he saw if they had been confirmed. If they hadn't, he would administer the sacrament there and then.

Cantelupe would have continued to lead a blameless apostolic life, had it not been for his conflict with Archbishop John Pecham over what was, to him, the sacred cow of ecclesiastical jurisdiction. In 1282, having removed himself to Normandy, he found himself excommunicated by Pecham and took himself off to Rome to plead the justice of his cause to Pope Martin IV. Sadly, Cantelupe, already an old man of 64, was worn out by his journey and the punishing heat. He died and was buried in Orvieto.

◆

John Pecham, 1240–1292 *Archbishop of Canterbury*

A devout Englishman and Archbishop of Canterbury (1279–1292) who campaigned tirelessly against oppression and poverty, John Pecham managed to retain the favour of the king. This was no mean feat, considering he wasn't Edward I's preferred candidate for the archbishopric and was always a vigorous advocate for papal primacy. During his first council on arrival in England, Pecham invited controversy by including a provision that a copy of the Magna Carta be hung in all cathedrals and collegiate churches: a political action that seemed to invite the king's ire – yet, incredibly, there was no Henry II/Thomas Becket-style meltdown. Edward was even known to use the archbishop on diplomatic missions thereafter.

As archbishop, he was respected for his pious attributes, but his insistence on discipline and reform, fighting plurality (whereby one cleric held two or more benefices – church posts with financial benefits – at once) and monastic laxity, and applying such reform with a 'spot-check' system of sudden visitations, often offended contemporaries. Nonetheless, he was famous even at the time for his unswerving integrity, strict observance of the Franciscan rule and as an 'excellent maker of songs'.

◆

Thomas Netter, 1375–1430   *Thomas Waldensis*

Often referred to as Thomas Waldensis (he was born in Saffron Walden, Essex), Thomas Netter was the theologian, heretic-prosecutor and royal confessor who held the dying Henry V in his arms, and was the trusted tutor of that ruler's heir. His first three decades were steeped in the teaching of the Carmelites, embracing the full spectrum of learning at Oxford, from philosophy to Church law.

Following a brief period of ecumenical service in Italy, he changed course on his return to England, taking a prominent part in the prosecution of Wycliffites and Lollards, writing copiously on the subject of such heresies and presiding over the 'celebrity' trials of notorious Lollards Sir John Oldcastle and William White. He also travelled on diplomatic embassies on behalf of the king, during which he founded several Carmelite convents in Prussia and was styled the Apostle of Lithuania for his alleged conversion of Vitort, the heathen grand duke, to Christianity.

Netter was a strict reformer, yet was recorded as being kind, even tender, to those around him. After Henry V died in his arms, he became unofficial tutor to the infant Henry VI, and has been credited with fostering the young ruler's remarkable piety. On a trip abroad with the king he was taken ill and died, apparently in the 'odour of sanctity'.

◆

CHAPTER IV

BISHOPS: FROM FIGHTING
TO FRANKLY CORRUPT

Odo of Bayeux, 1036–1097   *William the Conqueror's half-brother*

Half-brother to William the Conqueror and the man responsible for commissioning the famous Bayeux Tapestry, Odo of Bayeux is nevertheless a bishop about whom little good is recorded by his ecclesiastical peers. Although ordained as a Christian cleric, it is said that Bayeux was greedy and ruthless in his quest for power and that he gained his vast wealth through corruption, extortion and outright robbery. At one point he was second only to the king in wealth and power in England.

Nonetheless, he contributed over 100 ships to William's invasion fleet and fought at the Battle of Hastings. As a reward, he was awarded land in 23 counties, primarily in the South East and in East Anglia, and was an entrenched royal minister, serving virtually as regent during William's many absences. There were times when he led the royal forces against rebellions. Yet Bayeux was universally disliked. When he suddenly fell from favour in 1082 – rumour has it that he secretly planned a military expedition to Italy in the aim of making himself pope – he was thrown into prison.

He remained there for the next five years until being reluctantly freed by William on his deathbed. No sooner was he out of prison than he was organising a rebellion against the new monarch, William II, in favour of his older Norman brother, Robert Curthose.

He escaped from the ashes of this uprising with William to live out the rest of his life in Curthose's Norman court. No one in England mourned his absence, but history has been a little kinder, noting his generous patronage in education, architecture and, allegedly, an early version of the *Song of Roland* (the oldest major work of French literature). Ever the man for a good profitable fight, Bayeux died in Sicily in 1097 on his way to the First Crusade.

Ranulf, 1060–1128   *'The flaming one'*

Colourful and incendiary from the moment he left Normandy and entered William I's court, Ranulf was soon given the nickname 'Flambard' – the flaming one – by his envious fellow courtiers. Alongside his reputation for mischief-making and rapacious extortion, Ranulf soon carved out a niche as an acute financier. For him, royal employment and personal profiteering always went hand-in-hand.

Under William, Ranulf was involved in drawing up the famous Domesday surveys. A chronicle of the time accused him of measuring England with a rope in his greedy rush to reassess royal dues. However, it was under William II that Flambard's flame burned the brightest and, in Flambard, William had found a henchman as predatory as himself in the profiteering from both Crown and Church.

In the early 1090s, Ranulf obviously decided that the way ahead was through the Church, so he extricated himself from his marriage, marrying off his wife Aelfgifu to a well-off Huntingdon merchant. He then concentrated on amassing a fortune through a slew of benefices and, by 1099, had put the gloss of respectability on his venal endeavours by obtaining for himself the wealthy See of Durham. However, the gravy train came to a halt when William was killed and Henry I took the throne. Ranulf then earned for himself the peculiar merit of not only being the very first prisoner of the then only partially completed Tower of London, but also the first to escape from it. Popular legend had him shinning down a rope smuggled to him by friends in a cask of wine. He fled to Normandy and into the service of Henry's brother and arch-enemy Robert Curthose, becoming one of his key advisers and urging him to invade England to press his claim for the English throne.

After the failed coup attempt of 1101 and Henry's defeat of Curthose in Normandy in 1106, Ranulf was among the first to make his peace with the

English monarch, but the best he could hope for was a restoration of his bishopric in Durham. So he stepped down from political life and retired to the North where, for a while, his reputation was further enlivened by scandalous tales of his approach to monastic life: good living, womanising and blatant nepotism. He purchased benefices for two of his sons before they were even out of their teens.

But his restless energy also stretched to bringing stability to Durham's finances, completing the cathedral that was started by his predecessor, fortifying the city of Durham, building Norham Castle, founding Mottisfont Priory and endowing the College of Christchurch in Hampshire. When he died in 1128, Ranulf's zest for life had its admirers. His death, said one local chronicler, had brought an end to the 'golden age, under Ranulf our bishop'.

◆

Roger of Salisbury, d. 1139   *Bishop of Salisbury*

As fast tracks to success in the medieval age go, that of Roger of Salisbury must be among the more eccentric. He was priest of a small chapel near Caen when future English ruler Henry I happened to hear mass there one day. Suitably impressed by the sheer speed with which Salisbury galloped through the service, Henry I took him on and brought him to England.

Having shown a flair for administration, bureaucracy and crowd-pleasing, Salisbury was given England's chancery almost as soon as Henry was enthroned. Soon after he became the Bishop of Salisbury. The diocese had to wait, however, because Salisbury was busy at a national level, completely remodelling the exchequer system (which was subsequently managed by him and his family for nearly a century) and proving just as efficient and innovative at building up his own wealth. Both were to prove crucial in the anarchy that followed Henry's death.

Having originally sworn allegiance to the king's daughter Matilda, Salisbury defected to the future King Stephen in 1135, taking with him both the royal treasure and administrative power.

Salisbury enjoyed Stephen's complete dependence on him and also on his son and nephews, all of whom were bishops themselves. At one point the king declared that if Salisbury demanded half his kingdom he should have it, and the old bishop was said to have behaved as if he were the king's equal. Eventually, however, the sheer weight of Salisbury's dominance unnerved Stephen and a council called by the king demanded Salisbury's arrest and the confiscation of his family's castles.

Violence to men of the cloth was considered an unpardonable crime by Salisbury's fellow clergymen and they decided to 'turn coat' and support the claims of Matilda over the ruling Stephen. Unfortunately, Salisbury was unable to gloat at the result; he died in 1139, just as the country tipped over into a civil war that would end in Stephen's eventual humiliation.

◆

Baldwin of Ford, d. 1190   *Archbishop of Canterbury*

Having initially rejected a career path through the clergy in favour of living a simple monastic life, Baldwin of Ford still managed to rise to the top by becoming Bishop of Worcester and then Archbishop of Canterbury under the rule of Richard I.

Modest, ascetic and deliberate in all of his dealings, there wasn't a word said against Ford – and therein lay his ultimate failure. Once raised to great power, the very kindliness and mildness that had recommended him thus far was diluted into weak, ineffectual laxness.

As one chronicler noted, Baldwin was given to 'acting more like a mother offering her breasts than a father wielding his rod'. This approach spelled disaster and soon the Church lost all sense of discipline. In one of the most pithy papal greetings ever, his governance was summed up in a letter from Pope Urban which said: 'Urban, bishop, servant of the servants of God, sends his greetings to the most fervent monk, the warm abbot, the lukewarm bishop, the negligent archbishop.'

◆

Hugh du Puiset, 1120–1195   *Hugh 'Pudsey'*

Despite being the nephew of King Stephen and quickly rising through the ranks of the Church, Hugh du Puiset was more prosaically known by contemporaries as Hugh 'Pudsey'. He had been brought to England by the Blois monarchy and appointed Bishop of Durham in 1153, despite the opposition of the Archbishop of York.

Initially keeping out of the limelight, Du Puiset survived any fallout between the different regimes of kings Stephen and Henry II, remaining in the north of England and keeping busy with diocesan issues, amassing huge wealth and having a long affair with Alice de Percy, a local noblewoman.

He remained neutral during the conflict between Henry II and Thomas Becket, but inexplicably let himself become involved with the rebellion of

Henry's sons and wife, Eleanor, in 1173–4. When it failed, he was forced to surrender the See of Durham and had to rely on the patronage of the pope for his political survival.

Du Puiset only returned to power when Richard I ascended the throne in 1189 and sold various offices. Together with his old seat at Durham, Du Puiset bought the earldom of Northumberland which, given that the Archbishopric of York had been deliberately left vacant since 1181, transformed him into one of the most powerful bishops of that period. So imagine his annoyance when the York vacancy was filled. He was later ousted from his earldom and died while petitioning to Richard for its return.

◆

William Longchamp, d. 1197 *Chancellor of England*

C alled a son of two traitors by Henry II, Normandy-born William Longchamp didn't let the king's dislike for him prevent his rapid rise through the Angevin bureaucracy. When Richard I inherited the throne, he made Longchamp Chancellor of the Kingdom and Bishop of Ely. During the Lionheart's long absences Longchamp was made joint justiciar, along with Hugh du Puiset. Longchamp was not, however, a man who liked to share power.

Within just 18 months, he had ousted Du Puiset and managed to inveigle a commission to be papal legate for Pope Celestine. For the next three years, he was master of both state and Church in England. However, he was widely maligned as a result of his disagreeable manners, his utter disdain for all things English and his contemptuous pride.

Longchamp's unpopularity was such that even Prince John seemed preferable, giving the possible heir the opportunity to pose as the champion of English interests against the hated Frenchman. Things reached a head in 1192 when Longchamp, having barricaded himself into the Tower of London, was forced out by an unlikely alliance of John, various barons and a commune of London citizens. He escaped the country dressed as a woman.

Clawing back from this brink, Longchamp managed to restore himself to royal favour by getting King Richard to believe that it was he who had fixed a settlement releasing Richard from his German captivity. Clearly always the able diplomat, for the rest of the Lionheart's reign Longchamp was employed in delicate diplomatic missions for Richard until he died in 1197.

◆

St Hugh, 1135–1200 *Bishop of Lincoln*

Born in France, St Hugh's mother died when he was just eight and his father retired into monastic life taking his son with him. Hugh did well as a monk and, in 1179, was sent to become Prior of Witham in Somerset, England's first Carthusian monastery (the founding of which had been Henry II's self-imposed penance for the death of Becket).

For Hugh, royal advancement was no barrier to principle. Even when the king rewarded his service with the influential Bishopric of Lincoln, Hugh didn't dilute his often trenchant criticism of the king. He upbraided him for keeping church offices vacant so that the Crown could profit from them, excommunicated a royal forester for mistreating a citizen of

Lincoln and refused to allow Henry to choose his underlings in Lincoln. Describing himself as having a temper 'more biting than pepper', such was Hugh's charm and obvious diplomacy that he got away with it. One biographer wrote that when it came to Henry II, 'of all men only Hugh could bend that rhinoceros to his will'. Later on, he even refused to raise money for Richard the Lionheart's foreign wars. He was a model bishop: legendarily generous and approachable, nursing lepers, rebuilding Lincoln Cathedral, supporting education and protecting the Jews, great numbers of whom lived in Lincoln, against persecution during the early years of Richard I's reign.

Legend has it that he was accompanied everywhere by the white swan of Stow (which became his emblem) which guarded him while he slept. At his funeral, King John himself helped to carry his coffin to its resting place in Lincoln Cathedral. Hugh was canonized only 20 years after his death.

◆

Richard Poore, d. 1237   *Bishop of Salisbury*

When his brother Herbert died in 1217, Richard Poore, then Bishop of Chichester, succeeded to his late brother's position as Bishop of Salisbury. Dynastic office-holding notwithstanding, Poore made his own mark while bishop, as the man who started the construction of the great new Salisbury Cathedral. Laying the first foundation stones in April 1220, well away from the previous structure at Old Sarum, Poore wanted the new church to be built with an exceptional (and rare) architectural unity and it took over half a century to complete. Yet this wasn't Poore's only contribution to medieval England. Some consider him to be the author of *Ancrene Riwle*, the greatest prose text of the time, which describes the lifestyle and privations of anchorites, those holy men who were confined to a cell for lifelong devotion. Poore ended his own devotions in Durham, where he commissioned the great Chapel of the Nine Altars in Durham Cathedral.

◆

Walter de Merton, 1205–1277   *Chancellor and Bishop of Rochester*

In 1261, when the prosperous clerk and recently appointed Chancellor Walter de Merton set aside two manors in Surrey for the priory in his hometown of Merton, to support 'scholars residing at the schools', no one could have imagined that this action would lead to the start of the Oxford collegiate system, a university system subsequently copied and admired all over the world. But his patronage of education aside, De Merton was no model of piety, but a consummate career churchman.

His founding of Oxford's first college was to be the high point of his ecclesiastical achievement in a career that was otherwise subject to the vagaries of the secular world. He served Henry III as chancellor in the early 1260s, but was removed when the barons triumphed in 1263. He was reinstated as a justiciar in 1271 after the civil war, and was then made chancellor again on Henry III's death in 1272. He was regarded by then as a safe pair of hands. For the first two years of Edward I's reign he was virtually regent, but when Edward returned from the crusades he was ousted in favour of Robert Burnell, the pay-off being the Bishopric of Rochester.

It was in his constant to-ing and fro-ing between his fledgling college in Oxford and the diocesan duties in Kent that De Merton met his end.

While fording the River Medway, he fell from his horse and died from the effects two days later. Even though he was still a recent appointee to the See of Rochester, he was buried in Rochester Cathedral with full pomp. Valued at today's prices, his estate was worth around £45 million, much of which was bestowed to Merton College, thereby ensuring its survival in perpetuity.

◆

Robert Burnell, d. 1292   *Bishop of Bath and Wells*

A trained and skilful lawyer, Robert Burnell was Edward I's right-hand man. He was his regent during the two-year hiatus between Henry III's death and Edward's return from the Holy Land, and, on his return, Edward's chancellor. Edward tried twice to have his favourite appointed Archbishop of Canterbury, but failed both times. As a result, Burnell had to content himself with the bishopric of Bath and Wells.

As well as amassing a staggering personal wealth (he left estates in Worcestershire, Surrey, Somerset, Shropshire and Kent), he served Edward well. He provided the impetus behind the legislative reforms and acts that Edward's domestic regime is now famous for (they dropped off almost entirely after Burnell's death, almost 20 years into Edward's reign). He also helped direct the king's policy in France, Scotland and Wales and during that time actually spoke on the king's behalf on several public occasions.

In addition to all this, he also housed a parliamentary council at his house at Acton and was responsible for the permanent establishment of the Court of Chancery in London.

Anthony Bek, 1284–1311 *Bishop of Durham*

Anthony Bek, the Bishop of Durham, favoured Auckland Palace over Durham Castle as his main residence because of its proximity to the hunting grounds of Weardale, which perfectly exemplifies his priorities. At first, there wasn't even the pretence of piety about Bek, who was thrust upon the monks of Durham by Edward I. The splendour of his court was renowned: nobles had to address him from a kneeling position and, instead of mere servants, Bek was waited on at table by full knights.

His arrogance knew no bounds: he ignored the protests of his own monks, played fast and loose with the overriding authority of the Archbishop of York and, when the archbishop threatened to excommunicate him, appealed to the king that no mere archbishop had any right to punish a prince bishop without royal permission. Luckily for Bek, fortunate timing meant his one skill – military expertise – became a crucial commodity. He put down a rising on the border with Scotland, and a grateful king ensured that his career survived.

◆

Walter Langton, d. 1321 *Treasurer of England*

In a rollercoaster career that peaked when he was Treasurer of England and ended in obscurity in his diocese of Lichfield, Walter Langton seemed powerless to resist the swings and roundabouts of the politics and intrigues surrounding him. One minute he was the favourite of Edward I and reaping a clutch of benefices, becoming treasurer in 1295 and Bishop of Lichfield in 1296; the next, he was cold-shouldered by jealous barons and accused of murder, adultery and simony (the buying or selling of ecclesiastical pardons, offices or emoluments). When Edward II acceded to the throne, his lands – and huge hoard of moveable wealth – were seized amid accusations of venality and Langton was sent to prison.

Eventually released in 1312, Langton again became treasurer but, incredibly, managed to fall out once again with his peers, the Ordainers. This time, Archbishop of Canterbury, Winchelsea, was to prove no tactical saviour and he was excommunicated.

Langton did not return to England again until after Winchelsea's death in 1313 and served on the Royal Council until his dismissal at the request of parliament in 1315. He died in 1321 and was buried in Lichfield Cathedral, refurbished and enriched at Langton's own expense. It was at last a permanent posting in the life of a man who seemed unable to remain in either power or obscurity.

◆

Adam Orleton, c. 1275–1345   *Bishop of Hereford*

As Bishop of Hereford during the reigns of Edward II and Edward III, Adam Orleton is a possible candidate for the villainous Bishop of Hereford who was later added to the legends of Robin Hood. According to the tales, Robin forced the bad bishop to conduct a mass for his soul, then humiliated him by making him dance in his boots.

In real life, not a great deal is known about Orleton. He came from exceptionally obscure roots, was one of the first bishops to be 'translated' (moved) from one see to another, but other than that, it is hard to see exactly what drew the particular odium implied by the association with

Robin. Orleton was industrious on several fronts – monastic reform, confirmations, the defence of Episcopal rights and in the civil service – but, according to one vitriolic (and therefore, possibly biased) chronicler, was charged with treason in 1322. Later he supported the rebellion by Edward II's wife, Isabella, and her lover, Roger Mortimer, and was implicated in Edward II's murder.

Philip Repingdon, d. 1424 *Bishop of Lincoln*

For a man who ended up being both a powerful bishop and a cardinal, Philip Repingdon (aka Repington or Repyngdon) had a shaky start. He fell in with Wycliffites at the start of his clerical life and was actually excommunicated in 1382 when he was still in his 20s. Recanting his heretical views, he soon got into his stride within the Church establishment, becoming abbot of his monastery, and then a regular Chancellor of Oxford University. On the accession of Henry IV, court life called. He was extremely close to the young Henry Bolingbroke and, once Henry became monarch, became his chaplain and most intimate confessor.

He was rewarded with the Bishopric of Lincoln in 1404 and, four years later, was made a cardinal by Pope Gregory XII. Unfortunately, papal appointments were only as good as the person who made them. First Gregory was deposed and Repingdon's cardinalcy was invalidated, then he was reinstated a year later.

For the next 10 years, Repingdon managed to juggle the different demands of his episcopacy at Lincoln with a papacy master, but in 1419, he resigned Lincoln and retired from public life until his death five years later. Repingdon was famous for the quality of his sermons; manuscripts of which some have survived and can be found in the libraries of Oxford, Cambridge and London.

William Lyndwood, 1375–1446   *Bishop of St David's*

Chiefly remembered for his *Provinciale* – a comprehensive commentary on the peculiarities of English ecclesiastical law at that time and a faithful picture of the views and attitudes of the English clergy (which became one of the first books to be printed in England) – William Lyndwood was also a distinguished career clergyman.

Having risen through the ranks to become a long-standing Keeper of the Privy Seal (number three in the ministerial power structure), Henry VI himself recommended Lyndwood for the Bishopric of St David's. He was closely associated with Archbishop Henry Chichele in his trials of leading Lollards, but was more often sent abroad by the king on diplomatic missions, taking a prominent part as negotiator in political and commercial treaties. He was buried in St Stephen's, Westminster. In 1852, his body was found wrapped in a shroud and almost without any signs of corruption. This was testament, some said, to his reputation as 'head and shoulders above other bishops' of the 14th and 15th centuries.

◆

Henry Beaufort, 1376–1447   *Bishop of Lincoln*

Beaufort stands out from the mass of self-promoting bishops in a number of ways. First and foremost he was born – on the wrong side of the blanket – exceptionally close to the throne. Second, he was never afraid to nail his colours to a political mast, and third, he was one of the greatest royal creditors of the 15th century. He lent hundreds of thousands of pounds to the succession of Henrys that came to and departed from the English throne.

As the second son of John of Gaunt and his mistress Katherine Swynford, Henry and the rest of the Beauforts were legitimised by Richard II in 1397. But illegitimacy hadn't prevented Beaufort from already amassing great power and wealth. While he was still attending Oxford and Cambridge universities, he was accumulating benefices. Even before his half-brother Henry IV took the throne, Beaufort had managed to snaffle the Bishopric of Lincoln. Later, in 1404, he gave up his royal appointment as chancellor to be translated to the even wealthier See of Winchester, a cash-cow that he held for 43 years even, unusually, while also serving as a cardinal for the last 20 years of his life.

Along the way, Beaufort proved himself an extremely skilled power-player in the highest echelons of administration. He was a trusted councillor to the Lancastrian dynasty, a person who dipped in and out of office almost as the fancy took him and, especially in his later years, a deft diplomat overseas who worked as a papal legate in Germany, Hungary and Bohemia, assisting the pope in the Hussite War.

When war broke out with France, under his nephew Henry V, Beaufort constantly confirmed his value to his country with large financial advances. Reputedly, it was also Beaufort who developed the myth of Agincourt as the sign from above of a 'higher' destiny for England, stiffening the sinews of an already muscular monarchy.

◆

Reginald Pecock, 1395–1460   *Bishop of Chichester*

escribed by historians as 'the only great English theologian of the 15th century', in attacking the Lollards, Reginald Pecock aired religious views that were far in advance of his time. On its own, this might not have excited comment, but this was during the Wars of the Roses when even the most pious and unworldly churchman couldn't escape some sort of political taint.

In Pecock's case, having written respected treatises on means by which the laity might be corrected and brought into line with the Church, his very mention of the laity was seen as 'pandering' to them by the Church hierarchy. Worse was his theological debate on whether or not natural law overrode the authority of the scriptures or the Church. Still, he might have survived had it not been for the fact he was linked to the unpopular Duke of Suffolk, one of whose last acts before his assassination was to procure the Bishopric of Chichester for Pecock, thereby tying the clergyman to the falling star of Lancaster.

With the Yorkists in ascendance in the late 1450s, the Archbishop of Canterbury was able to sentence Pecock on the grounds of heresy to either complete public recanting or death at the stake. On 4 December 1457, at St Paul's Cross, Pecock privately, then publicly, renounced his entire lexicon of opinions, including a list of errors most of which he had neither held nor taught. He was unceremoniously forced to resign his bishopric and confined to Thorney Abbey in Cambridgeshire, where he sank into obscurity and, presumably, died.

◆

William Wayneflete, 1395–1486   *Provost of Eton*

F amous as the first headmaster of Eton College, it seems that William Wayneflete himself (aka William Barbour) started out as a needy scholar, probably a grammar-school boy, before going to Oxford

University. His translation from being headmaster at the already well-respected Winchester College to the headship of Eton was undoubtedly a last-minute whim of a youthful Henry VI. Having spent a weekend there to see the school for himself in July 1441, the 20-year-old Henry seems to have poached Wayneflete almost immediately. By Christmas 1442 he was installed at Eton, having accepted a royal livery – about five yards of violet cloth – as Provost of Eton.

Over the next few years, Wayneflete populated the new school with pupils from Winchester, cemented the links between Eton and Henry VI's other foundation, King's College at Cambridge (so that the latter recruited entirely from the former), and founded and built his own college, Magdalen, at Oxford.

Along the way he managed to avoid the political pitfalls of Cade's Rebellion in 1450 and the later Wars of the Roses. In 1467, he became chancellor and died still serving the monarchy at the age of 88. His long life had spanned the reigns of no less than eight English monarchs: Richard II, Henrys IV, V, VI, Edwards IV and V, Richard III and Henry VII.

◆

John Morton, 1420–1500   *Archbishop of Canterbury*

Standing initially as an implacable foe of the Yorkists, Morton was surprisingly prominent in the last years of Edward IV, being given the profitable Bishopric of Ely in 1479 and made an executor of Edward IV's will. On Richard III's accession Morton was arrested and, after Buckingham's revolt, fled to France and then to the camp of Henry Tudor, hence his later favour with Henry: he became Archbishop of Canterbury, chancellor and a cardinal, all within 10 years of Henry VII's accession to the throne. Rooted in the medieval age, however, were two longer-lasting legacies for which he is still remembered today.

The first was his *History of Richard III*, which was originally ascribed to Sir Thomas More. This was the fable on which Shakespeare based his depiction of the last Yorkist monarch, and which still informs our view of Richard III as a grotesque, deformed, blacker-than-black villain. The second is the axiom 'Morton's fork'. This was originally a policy of tax collection formulated by Morton from his long experience as a medieval administrator and put into action when he became chancellor.

If the subject lived in luxury, and had clearly spent a lot of money on himself, then he obviously had sufficient income to spare some for the king. If, on the other hand, the subject lived frugally and showed no signs of outward wealth, then he must have substantial savings, out of which he could then afford to give some to the king. These arguments were known as the 'two prongs of Morton's fork', which became an expression analogous to 'catch-22' or 'between a rock and a hard place'.

◆

THE THINKING MAN'S CHOICE: MEN OF SCIENCE & FACT

Henry of Huntingdon, c. 1080–1155 *Historian*

When asked by Bishop Alexander of Lincoln to compile a history of England, using the texts of the Venerable Bede as groundwork, Henry of Huntingdon (then the Archdeacon of Huntingdon) more than fulfilled his brief with the *Historia Anglorum*, starting with the Roman invasion of 43BC and culminating (almost up to Huntingdon's own deathbed) with the accession of Henry II in 1154. Although nearly three quarters of it derives directly from the work of others, Huntingdon's first-hand knowledge spans the years 1126–1154, the reigns of Henry I and Henry II, and the anarchic period of Stephen and Matilda.

Altogether, the *Historia Anglorum* is renowned for its colourful and dramatic tone – for example, the spectacularly revolting description of Henry I's rotting corpse – it was backed up by rigorous research and a careful political agenda. It puts the ethnicity and nationality issues of Huntingdon's time into context and, essentially, justifies the rule of the Normans over the English.

◆

William of Malmesbury, c. 1080–1143 *Historian*

Contemporaneous with Henry of Huntingdon, William of Malmesbury is the Normans' Kenneth Clarke (of *Civilisation* fame) to Henry's Simon Schama: both were popular, but with Malmesbury winning the toss as the more heavyweight of the two. Trained in the famous Malmesbury Abbey in logic, physics and moral philosophy, William produced a wide-ranging body of work, which included, in 1120, the *Gesta Regum Anglorum*

(*Deeds of the English Kings*). This is now considered to be one of the greatest histories of England ever written and is seen as a fulfilment of his belief that history was a strand of moral philosophy. How this translates to the page is seen in the way Malmesbury sticks to the principle of recounting events to show their cause and effect, rather than just rattling off the facts.

More strongly than most historians of the medieval age, Malmesbury was also prepared to speculate on human motivation, such as when he suggests that when Pope Urban II launched the First Crusade it was just a ruse to grab back papal lands. When woven in with some shrewd and vivid anecdotes about the people and events of his time, the result was compelling enough to ensure Malmesbury's accounts were studied down the ages.

The fact he was sycophantic to whichever ruler he was writing under, was anti-Semitic in his comments on the Jewish population in England and was hilariously scornful of life's fripperies just makes him a man of his age. What was startling – and was his lasting legacy – was his ambivalence on the Norman-English question, thereby restoring an English past (and pride) to his Anglo-Norman readership and to those that studied him in the centuries after.

◆

Adelard of Bath, c. 1080–1160   *Scientist*

Adelard of Bath was often called the first English scientist, the Indiana Jones of the medieval age, actively seeking out knowledge by travelling for nearly a decade in the often dangerous reaches of Greece and Asia Minor, and being one of the first thinkers of the time to make a wholesale translation of Arabo-Greek learning directly from Arabic into Latin. Born in Bath, Adelard was educated in Tours from 1100, where he once played the cithar (a forerunner to the guitar) to Matilda, Henry I's queen, during which a little boy became so carried away that he waved his arms around with wild enthusiasm, reducing the royal entourage to giggles.

Royal patronage may have helped Adelard to travel to Sicily, Greece, Spain, Italy, what we would now call the Middle East and, probably, North Africa, only returning to England in 1116. Initially, it wasn't a joyful homecoming. He wrote of his fellow Englishmen that: 'Its chief men are violent, its magistrates wine-lovers, its judges mercenary, its patrons fickle, its private men sycophants, those who make promises deceitful, friends full of jealousy and almost all men self-seekers.'

Still, he based himself in Bristol and Bath, and assembled an incredible body of work: astrology, astronomy, philosophy and mathematics, and he often put an original spin on the works he was translating. For example, *Natural Questions* (c. 1133), an anthology of Arabic studies, takes the form of a conversation between himself and a nephew, where Adelard proffers his own belief that the Earth is round, muses about how it was stationary in space and flirts with the idea of gravity in his exploration into how far a rock would fall if dropped into a hole drilled through the Earth.

His translations of Euclid's *Elements* were, for centuries, the main geometry textbooks in the West; he brought to his Latin-reading audience the abacus, the navigational and time-keeping astrolabe and the 'zero'; he wrote on falconry and homeopathy; and he prepared royal horoscopes. Such intellect and self-confidence enabled Adelard to state, without fear of carping from the Church, that he preferred reason to authority and that there need be no conflict between science and religion. It is not known exactly when he died, or where he is buried.

Geoffrey of Monmouth, c. 1100–1155 *Historian*

ne of the great legend-makers of all time, along with Henry of Huntingdon and William of Malmesbury, Geoffrey of Monmouth rounds off our trio of post-Conquest chroniclers. With *Historia Regum Britanniae* (*History of the Kings of Britain*) he earns his place in the pantheon, but not for historical woolgathering: rather for creating one of the most influential books ever to come out of Britain, a daring, spectacular work. It claimed to relate the history of Britain up to as far as the 7th century, before the arrival of the English, but was almost, as one historian said, a deliberate spoof, a cunning ploy to fill a gap in the market of histories extant.

Monmouth's *History* is packed with colourful legends (such as the one of King Lear and his daughters) which he claimed to have extracted from 'a most ancient book' from either Brittany or Wales, and written so convincingly that, for years, Monmouth's works were used for reference purposes across the continent.

With his evocative tales adding flesh to the bones of the story of King Arthur and Merlin, he established the chivalric Arthurian tradition, and stepping into his footsteps over the years were men like Sir Thomas Malory, Alfred, Lord Tennyson, William Shakespeare, John Milton, John Dryden and William Wordsworth.

Monmouth's own life was not as romantic as his writing. From teaching at Oxford and moving in court circles, he might have been disappointed by only receiving the straitened See of St Asaph (for which he'd been ordained only days before, aged 42). He certainly never entered the diocese. After his death in 1155, the Welsh adopted his *History* for their own ends, as proof of their fated return to power in their own country, until the accession of Henry Tudor to the English throne part-satisfied their epic ambitions.

Robert Grosseteste, c. 1175–1253 *Scientist*

ad name, brilliant man. Eclipsed by the scholars that came before and after him in terms of renown, humble of birth, reputedly ignorant of both Greek and Hebrew, and often distracted by his zeal for reform and his involvement with the politics of the day, Robert Grosseteste is nonetheless credited by historians as being 'the real founder of the tradition of scientific thought in medieval Oxford and, in some ways, of the modern English intellectual tradition', England's first real mathematician and physicist of his age.

Although he spent much of his life in Oxford, as a teacher and rector of the first Franciscan school there, Grosseteste wore his learning lightly. His reputation as an original thinker survives, with works on geometry, optics, logic, tides and even rainbows. Alongside such vision, Grosseteste maintained a flourishing political career. As Bishop of Lincoln for 18 years, he was in charge of England's largest diocese, which reached from the Humber to the Thames and, in a litigious and turbulent age of power struggles, stood out for the tenaciousness and breadth of his reforms there.

He was equally fearless on the national stage. Grosseteste foiled a bid by the king to divide and conquer his foes in 1244 by separating the legislative powers of the clergy from those of the baronage; in 1251 he protested against a papal mandate commanding the English clergy to pay Henry III a tenth of their revenues for a crusade, and a political tract written by him on the difference between a monarchy and a tyranny brought him into friendship with the baronial rebel Simon de Montfort. When he died he was between 70 and 80 years of age – a statesman of both Church and country.

◆

Gilbert 'the Englishman', c. 1180–1250   *Medical writer*

𝕿 he phrase 'look into my eyes' had a whole other implication in medieval England, as vividly illustrated by the medical *Compendium* (c. 1240) of Gilbert 'the Englishman', the country's first major medical writer. 'He whose eyes are large and tremulous is lazy and a braggart, and fond of women,' writes Gilbert, presumably with hard, narrowed eyes himself. Strange ocular judgements aside, all seven volumes of the vast *Compendium* display a giddying coverage of general diseases, just about every 'ology' you could care to name, a prevention for sea-sickness and even a discussion about cosmetics: the plethora of cures for wrinkles, age spots, moles, warts, bad breath and body odour would put a modern spa to shame.

Gilbert brought his experience of extensive travel, a thirst for reading and knowledge, clarity of expression and a dose of common sense and scepticism to his work. Despite treading a fine line between the then-taboo subject of surgery and ecclesiastically sanctioned medicine, Gilbert survived the strictures of the Church, even attending to the Archbishop of Canterbury on his deathbed; otherwise we know little about him. It is estimated he produced the *Compendium* around 1240 and died around 1250.

◆

Roger Bacon, 1214–1294   *Intellect and author*

𝕽 oger Bacon introduced gunpowder to the West, but never produced any. He invented spectacles without actually crafting a pair, and he anticipated later inventions such as steamships, telescopes, microscopes and flying machines. He recognised the visible spectrum in a glass of water, centuries before Sir Isaac Newton sorted out the prismatic qualities of light. He did not, as was rumoured, create a talking head made out of brass – the world's first robot – which could answer any question, but his contemporaries would not have been surprised if he had. If Bacon had actually moved beyond the theoretical to the practical, his discoveries would have catapulted England hundreds of years into the future.

As it was, he possessed one of the most outstanding intellects of his era, produced a staggering amount of written work and certainly earned his popular monicker of 'Doctor Mirabilis'. Apart from a short spell in Paris, he spent the first half of his life studying in Oxford, oblivious to much going on around him. He became a monk in the fairly new order of the Franciscans when he was already, by the standards of the time, an old man of 40. Then, in 1256, the outside world intruded. An old enemy became head of the Franciscans and moved Bacon out of Oxford to France, and out of the mainstream of intellectual life.

Hampered by the Franciscan prohibition on publishing works without the order's permission, Bacon was secretly supported in his running battle with his superiors by Pope Clement IV, to whom he sent his *Opus Majus*, *Opus Minus* and *Opus Tertium*, the wide-ranging trilogy of grammar, logic, mathematics, physics and philosophy that, together with his planned encyclopaedia of the entire natural world, are his greatest achievements.

By the 1270s, the Franciscans had lost patience and Bacon was imprisoned for unorthodox teaching, heresy and even for largely unfounded suspicions of witchcraft in his treatise on alchemy. Despite all of this, he carried on writing through his 10-year imprisonment and right up until his death in 1294.

◆

Sir Thomas Gray, 1272–1369   *Historian*

When Sir Thomas Gray, a knight known for his bruising battles on the borders, was captured by the Scots and imprisoned in Edinburgh Castle in 1355, he didn't waste time counting his lice or dwelling on the prison menu. Instead, he bequeathed us the first-known historical chronicle in post-conquest England to have been written by a member of the lay nobility.

Spanning the history of England from the Creation to his present-day, and written in Anglo-Norman French, the *Scalacronica* (so-named because of the scaling ladder in the crest of the Grays, perhaps with a pun intended to signify England pulling herself out of barbarism) was the end result. The section from the reign of Edward I is, essentially, written from first-hand. It is based on Gray's and his father's own memories of their experiences in the Scottish campaigns and French wars and, as onlookers to the era's big events, so provides a unique perspective on the politics of the day and a colourful glimpse into the life of a knight.

◆

William Occam, 1288–1348   *Philosopher*

William Occam was among the most influential philosophers of the High Middle Ages, one of the era's greatest speculative minds and the most ascetic of Franciscan monks, the last of which qualities would, bizarrely, bring about his downfall.

As a rigorous logician he bequeathed us 'Occam's razor', which is the principle that, in explaining anything, no more explanation should be made than is absolutely necessary. Sadly, why a logical maxim should be named after a shaving tool doesn't seem to qualify for an explanation. Nor would the philosophical squabbles as to whether Occam was more a pioneer of conceptualism or a pioneer of nominalism. Luckily, it's generally accepted that Occam was the father of modern epistemology.

For a man with unknown beginnings, Occam's own career was rich in controversy. In concluding that theology was a question of faith and not proof, Occam wrote that reason, philosophy and the intellect had nothing to contribute to our knowledge of God, thereby rattling the very foundations of the previous centuries of Church-sponsored endeavour.

So novel were his views that he was summoned to the papal court in Avignon, where Pope John XXII was already suspicious of Occam's Franciscan views on the need for clergy to adhere to the idea of absolute poverty. When Occam concluded, in Avignon in 1328, that Pope John himself was a heretic in his refusal to embrace poverty, he was punished with excommunication and forced to flee.

He spent the remainder of his life as an anti-papal propagandist from the safety of Germany, where he died, having laid down the thoughts that would become the stepping stones towards Protestantism.

◆

Thomas Bradwardine, c. 1290–1349 *Theologian and mathematician*

Thomas Bradwardine was a crowning figure of the 'Oxford Calculators', that extraordinary intellectual surge of the 13th century, and a popular hero as well. When he accompanied Edward III as his chaplain and confessor for the campaigns of Crécy and Neville's Cross, such was his personal magnetism among the English soldiers that many ascribed the victories there to him. Chaucer coupled him with St Augustine and Boethius as a theologian, but it was as 'the Profound Doctor' that Bradwardine really shone. In astrophysics, he and his other Oxford Calculators hit upon the essence of the Law of Falling Bodies, long before Galileo, to whom we attribute this discovery. In mathematics, Bradwardine anticipated the concept of exponential growth and compound interest. In neither field did he quite make the breakthrough that might have placed him centre-stage in history, nor did his secular ambitions pan out. Edward III passed him over for the Archbishopric of Canterbury and only when the king's first choice died in the Black Death was Bradwardine eventually appointed by the pope in Avignon. But, he, too, succumbed to the plague, only 40 days after his consecration.

◆

Sir John Arderne, 1307–1392 *Surgeon*

With the Barber's Company off the ground in 1308, and established by ordinance in 1376, the divergence of surgery from medicine seemed set in stone. But in 1365, a small number of medically trained lay practitioners formed the Guild of Surgeons. This was a plucky move against the condemnation of surgery by the Church over a century before. In 1370, one of its members was the Newark-born Sir John Arderne, now considered one of the fathers of English surgery, with many of his treatments still in use today. Not only did he have revolutionary views on fees – that while wealthy men should be charged as much as they could afford, poor men should be cured free of charge – but he was also one of the first of his time to devise workable treatments for both diseases and wounds. On a more prurient note, he is especially well known for his recommendations for surgery to correct anal fistula, a disorder to which the English were thought to be prone, especially among knights, who developed these painful rectal abscesses due to the long periods they spent on horseback.

◆

Thomas Walsingham, d. 1422   *Historian*

espite spending his entire life as a monk at St Albans Abbey, Thomas Walsingham showed a particularly political awareness of which side his bread was buttered. In the six chronicles attributed to him, the trenchant criticisms of the second, *Chronicon Angliae*, about the character of John of Gaunt are almost entirely neutered in the fourth, a *Chronicle of St Albans*, which was written when John of Gaunt's son, Henry IV, was on the throne.

Political correctness aside, Walsingham's chronicles are among the most comprehensive and colourful to survive from medieval England. They cover half a century of turbulence, from the final years of Edward III, through the Peasants' Revolt, the murder of Richard II, the final stand of the Welsh and Henry V's glorious victory at Agincourt. The gathering of historical fact is painstaking, dependable and often unique in the sheer wealth of detail – we owe Walsingham for much of our knowledge of Wycliffe and the Lollards – which made it so useful for William Shakespeare when he came to write his slew of plays dealing with Walsingham's period.

CHAPTER VI

◆

BARONS & BIG CHEESES

Robert, 1104–1168 & Waleran, 1104–1166   *The Beaumont twins*

In an era of rebellion, the cliché of a titanic struggle between the liege lord and his bumptious barons is one we are all familiar with. But the nobles were not always pitted against kings. In some cases, there was a happy marriage of mutual self-interest and loyalty, to the advantage of both master and minion.

Left fatherless as infants, the Beaumont twins were brought up at the court of Henry I, inseparable and precocious. As teenagers, they were said to have charmed the socks off a council of cardinals in 1119 with their breadth of knowledge. Present at Henry I's deathbed, they plumped for Stephen in 'the anarchy' and became his chief advisers in return for large grants of land. Waleran especially flourished, becoming, as one historian described, 'possibly the most important man in England after the king', and was crucial in ensuring the continued allegiance of Normandy to the more up-and-coming English nation.

Unfortunately, Waleran's compulsive intriguing and politicking got him into hot water. To save his French estates in 1141 he made a treaty with Empress Matilda and left Stephen's England, never to return. Even back in Normandy, his influence there began to wane. By 1153, Waleran was out of the limelight permanently, which is where he stayed until his death in 1166.

Meanwhile, younger twin Robert had been no slouch. Despite being in Waleran's shadow at the start of Stephen's reign, he had built up a network of influence and power that, by the mid-1150s, as lifelong justiciar under Henry II, made him the grand old man of the English baronage.

Calm and discreet where his brother was known to be impulsive and vain, Robert was Henry's closest confidant, regularly left in charge of the country when Henry was fighting abroad. His rewards for such excellent royal service? Estates that stretched across the very heart of England – from Wales to Norfolk – and the self-satisfaction of having invested the post of justiciar with an importance that extended down the centuries.

◆

Ranulf III, 1170–1232 *Earl of Chester*

With estates in the north-east and north-west of England, Normandy and Brittany, Ranulf III was as rich in land and fortune as he was apparently lacking in height. Described as 'almost the last relic of the great feudal aristocracy of the conquest', Ranulf belonged to the traditional school of barons-as-paid-retainers, who saw themselves as a bulwark against the chaos of medieval England that then deserved rewards of status and wealth from their royal taskmasters.

Originally opposed to Prince John's attempt to seize the English throne in 1193–1194, Ranulf was initially only kept in line by John's blatant patronage once he was crowned. But in 1204, he was taking the king's tolerance for over-powerful behaviour to extremes. Arrested on suspicion of treatying with the Welsh with the intention of then rebelling himself, Ranulf had extensive estates in Cheshire temporarily confiscated. Ranulf wasn't stupid – he could read the writing on the wall and from then on, his relationship with John was very much more servile.

From 1209–1212, he battled tirelessly in the Welsh campaigns, helped negotiate the end of the papal interdict in 1213–1214, was loyal to John throughout the dealings over the Magna Carta (including leading the royalists to victory against his disgruntled fellow barons at Lincoln in 1217) and, as a postscript, oversaw the 1225 re-issue of the charter under a less-than-impressed Henry III. In return, John lavished him with royal patronage, including the earldom of Lincoln, a handful of shrievalties, and estates throughout the Midlands. He managed to maintain his influence as elder statesman after John's death, finally dying childless in 1232.

◆

Guy de Beauchamp, c. 1272–1315 *Earl of Warwick*

Named after *Gui de Warwic*, an Anglo-Norman romance supposedly written to flatter his grandfather back in the 1230s, Guy de Beauchamp, Earl of Warwick, had an embellished noble heritage and heroic bravura to live up to. He started well in his early 20s. He was intelligent, cultured and brave. He distinguished himself in the Scottish campaigns, starting at the Battle of Falkirk, for which he received vast tracts of Scottish land and married Alice, a Scots heiress, with whom he had six children in less than five years.

Even before Edward II came to the throne, De Beauchamp and Piers Gaveston, the prince's favourite, had fallen out. While strutting in victory after winning a jousting tournament, Gaveston sneered about his fellow barons that the Earl of Gloucester was a 'cuckold's bird', the Earl of Pembroke was 'Joseph the Jew' and that, because of his dark complexion, De Beauchamp should be known as 'the black dog of Arden'. De Beauchamp later said: 'If he calls me a dog, be sure that I will bite him so soon as I shall perceive my opportunity.' Thereafter, De Beauchamp was the only baron in permanent opposition to Edward II barracking for Gaveston's banishment both times. When Edward reneged the second time and brought Gaveston back in 1312, De Beauchamp seized Gaveston and set up a kangaroo court trial, but made himself absent from the actual execution.

Having been a supreme royal servant under Edward I, the die was now cast for De Beauchamp. He absented himself from Edward II's Bannockburn campaign, was a driving force behind the Ordinances drawn up by the barons to control Edward, and dominated the government until his premature death in 1315 (some say due to poison arranged by the vengeful king himself). Ironically, though, given his bitter opposition to Edward's favouritism, it was De Beauchamp who inadvertently helped forge the path of the next royal pet when the Despensers inherited estates from him.

◆

Humphrey de Bohun, 1276–1322   *4th Earl of Hereford*

ay 'Humphrey de Bohun' to a medievalist and they're likely to ask: 'Which one?' The family – eldest sons almost always called Humphrey – came to England with William the Conqueror. From then on, the De Bohuns were always connected with court, were careful to marry 'up' and increase their estates and were loyal to the throne. Only Edward II could have upset this apple-cart, and upset it he did, with his refusal to play ball with the established families and his wish to play less innocent games with new friends like Piers Gaveston.

Even though he was one of the barons who rebelled against Edward's blatant enslavement to Gaveston, De Bohun, the 4th Earl of Hereford, was married to Elizabeth, the king's sister, and was brought back into his brother-in-law's fold to fight at the battle of Bannockburn, where an act of bravery – he charged alone at Robert the Bruce – ended in his capture and ransom. Once released, De Bohun remained in the 'Middle Party' of baronial government, but was pushed into rebellion once more under the venal excesses of the Despensers.

Fighting against the royal forces at the Battle of Boroughbridge, De Bohun died a most excruciating death when a pikeman, concealed underneath a bridge across which the rebels were advancing, shoved his weapon up through the wood and skewered poor De Bohun through his anus. His screams of agony turned the advance into a panicked mêlée. It was the end for De Bohun and the beginning of the end for his comrades. Half a century on, the De Bohun name would die out, leaving only Mary, the wife of Henry IV, to maintain the family's importance.

◆

Thomas Plantagenet, 1278–1322 *2nd Earl of Lancaster*

Described by one commentator as 'the supreme example of the over-mighty subject', Thomas Plantagenet, 2nd Earl of Lancaster, would have seen himself more as a champion fighting a despotic government with the weapons of reform. As Henry III's grandson, Edward II's cousin and the husband of heiress Alice de Lacy, Plantagenet was the holder of five earldoms, making him one of the richest and most powerful men in England; his private army was mighty enough to sway matters of state and his annual income of £11,000 (nearly £4 million today) was greater than the king's. After the Piers Gaveston debacle, Guy de Beauchamp's and Plantagenet's absence from the Battle of Bannockburn forced Edward to eat humble pie. Thereafter, Plantagenet virtually ran the country until 1318.

Unfortunately, Plantagenet proved no better at governing than his cousin had, and when the increasing depredations of the Scots were too much for him, he was deposed by a new faction of barons. Soon the dreaded Despensers were in charge and Plantagenet found himself at the head of a baronial rebellion against them. He was defeated at the Battle of Boroughbridge in 1322, given a mock trial and then beheaded. With the exception of Gaveston who had been stripped of his title beforehand, Plantagenet was the first earl to be executed since the days of William the Conqueror.

In an unexpected footnote, within a few months of his death, Plantagenet was being hailed as a martyr, with miracles being witnessed at his tomb and his admirers clamouring for his canonization – certainly not the usual epitaph for a baron in the medieval age!

◆

John of Gaunt, 1340–1399 *Duke of Lancaster*

ick a title, any title, and John of Gaunt held it. Born (in Ghent, hence 'Gaunt') as the Earl of Richmond and princely third son of Edward III, he became Duke of Lancaster upon his marriage to wife Blanche, called himself King of Castile and Leon through his second wife, Constance of Castile, and, from 1394, gilded the rose with the title Duke of Aquitaine. His legitimate heirs – forming the House of Lancaster – included kings Henry IV, Henry V and Henry VI; his initially illegitimate offspring, the Beauforts, were without peer, their descendants becoming royal (Margaret Beaufort was Henry VII's mother) and going on to shine at the Tudor courts of the 16th century. Alongside this peerless pedigree came a reputation for honour, chivalry, dignity to the point of insufferability and, in the eyes of his critics, breathtaking arrogance.

While Lollards enjoyed his support, his vast slew of estates and a chain of 30 castles strung out across the country meant he had fingers in every county's pie. His wealth was legendary, his power undeniable, and his industry and hard work renowned, but there was also no small measure of skill in Gaunt's ability to make his influence over his father Edward III, then his nephew Richard II, look like devotion to the well-being of the kingdom rather than just self-aggrandisement. Even after a bad decade in the 1380s, when he was associated with the taxation hardships of Richard's minority and was even reputedly the object of an assassination attempt, Gaunt was able to claw back his credibility. On his return from an unsuccessful expedition to Castile, he was the only one able to bring about a compromise between a recalcitrant Richard and the Lords Appellant.

Having married his long-time love, Katherine, three years before, Gaunt died of natural causes in 1399 with her beside him. At the time, and looking at what was to come from his descendants, Gaunt was, as one commentator described 'the greatest noble in late medieval England'.

◆

Thomas Mowbray, 1366–1399   *Duke of Norfolk*

As a younger son, waiting in vain for a long-living grandmother to pass on his inheritance, Thomas Mowbray had to rely on ambition, a childhood spent with the king and a slippery gift for evading the consequences of his actions. Having had his nose put out of joint by

Richard II's favourite Robert de Vere, and then having been part of the original line-up of the Lords Appellant, formed to control the excesses of the king, Mowbray was quick to reconcile with the monarch and was returned to favour when Richard reached his majority in 1389.

By 1397, having successfully occupied various posts and commands, delicately helped to negotiate the king's second marriage, overseen the harrying and execution of his former comrades the Lords Appellant, and been awarded the dukedom of Norfolk, Mowbray was now one of England's most prominent nobles. One short year later, his star had plunged. Exiled for life, Mowbray died of the plague in Venice in 1399, at only 33 years old. This time, he had been unable to get himself out of a tricky situation. An argument with Henry Bolingbroke had escalated into banishment for them both. Bolingbroke retaliated by invading England and knocking Richard off the throne. Once installed on the throne as Henry IV, he was hardly likely to extend the hand of friendship to Mowbray, although when he heard of Mowbray's death in Venice, the king at least allowed his son to succeed to the earldom of Norfolk.

◆

Richard Neville, d. 1471   *16th Earl of Warwick*

An egotistical, selfish and over-powerful magnate, Richard Neville went down in history as 'Warwick the Kingmaker' with all its overtones of diplomacy and gravitas. Born the heir to the Earl of Salisbury, Neville inherited the earldom of Warwick through his wife, Anne de Beauchamp. This made him the richest man in England outside of the royal family and put him in the perfect position to influence affairs of state.

Throughout the chaos that was the Wars of the Roses, Neville was at the forefront of intrigues and alliances, initially on behalf of the Yorkists. In victory at the first battle of St Albans and at Northampton, and then in defeat at Wakefield or the second battle of St Albans, and before the final triumphs of Mortimer's Cross and Towton, Neville made himself indispensable to Edward of York. Or so he thought. Crowning Edward IV in 1461, Neville was now the most powerful man in England, and he could concentrate on his other areas of talent: matchmaking and diplomacy. However, he had gravely underestimated the new ruler's stubborn streak of independence.

Neville had intended his charge marry the King of France's sister-in-law, Bona of Savoy, but, in 1464, Edward announced he had married Elizabeth Woodville, favouring a Burgundian alliance over a French one. Having lost face with the French and with the court, a furious Neville now looked to the king's brother George, Duke of Clarence, as his next vehicle to greatness.

He married his daughter to George and financed his rebellion against Edward in 1469, but Neville had overestimated his new charge and the uprising proved a damp squib. Neville jumped ship and fled to France and was himself 'matchmade' by King Louis XI of France, into forming an alliance with the Lancastrian doyenne – and wife of the mentally absent Henry VI – Margaret of Anjou. It was an extraordinary U-turn. In 1470, at the head of a French and Lancastrian force, Neville invaded England. In the north, he had the Nevilles fighting for him, in the west, the Lancastrian earls. Together, they chased Edward IV into exile. Just as he had 'unmade' Henry VI years before, now Neville 'remade' him. But the restored regime was clutching at straws. It was unpopular, and both Neville and Margaret, the real powers behind the throne, were seen as opportunistic.

When Clarence broke ranks with the Lancastrians, peeved that Neville was now ingratiating himself with Prince Edward of Lancaster, Edward IV was able to return. At the final denouement at Barnet, it was a case of 'traitor meets trickster'. Neville was tricked onto the battlefield before his main forces arrived, by Edward IV, and was slain in the ensuing defeat. In the course of seven unlucky years, Neville had won and lost it all... and all over a failed marriage alliance.

◆

Henry Stafford, 1457–1483   *2nd Duke of Buckingham*

Although only related to the monarchy through the daughters of his younger sons, Henry Stafford still had his eyes on the throne. He didn't succeed for himself, but he did manage to put Richard III on the throne.

Inheriting as a toddler the headship of one of the wealthiest families of 15th-century England, Stafford increased his standing with his marriage to Edward IV's wife Elizabeth's sister. He was 12, she was 24, but the marriage was not a success. He wasn't trusted by Edward IV and was manoeuvred out of court influence, whereupon he threw his lot in with Richard, Duke of Gloucester.

Stafford was undoubtedly crucial in putting Richard III on the throne; he was instrumental in the imprisonment of young Edward V and his little brother, put the screws on the royal council to declare Edward IV's children illegitimate and rushed through the coronation of the new ruler. For this he was extraordinarily well-rewarded by Richard. He was instantly made High Steward and Constable of England, given the contested Bohun inheritance and, in an act of unparalleled delegation, the whole rule of Wales.

In this context, his next move – to revert to his Lancastrian roots in his apparent support of Henry Tudor and rebel against Richard – seems foolhardy. Unless, that is, you believe that he wanted the throne for himself, and that having set Richard up as murderer of the young princes and usurper of the throne, he then stirred up a Lancastrian rebellion to take it back from him. His plan might have succeeded, but Stafford's luck had run out. After a disastrous military campaign, he ran for his life, was turned in for the bounty Richard placed on him and was beheaded in Salisbury in November 1483. As the medieval age drew to a close, Stafford's ignominious end showed that the days of the over-mighty baron were finally numbered.

CHAPTER VII

◆

BEHIND THE SCENES:
MONEYLENDERS, MERCHANTS, PATRONS,
LAWMAKERS & CIVIL SERVANTS

Herfast, d. 1084   *Lord Chancellor*

As part of William the Conqueror's invasion force, Herfast was the backbone of the king's 'back office' and, in 1069, became the country's first lord chancellor. Like many a cautious civil servant since, Herfast saw no need for massive innovation in his role, so the English vernacular in royal writs was retained and Norman practices were minimised. But he was not so cautious in his own life. Despite being a clergyman, he seems to have been married and to have fathered a son and, in 1070, was lectured by Archbishop Lanfranc: 'Were you to devote less time to gambling and games of chance, to read the Bible for a change and to learn some canon law... you would cease to argue with your mother Church.'

◆

William Cade, d. 1166   *Financier*

One of the more shadowy figures of the 12th century was financier William Cade, who operated a vast circle of credit that involved everyone from monks and merchants right up to the monarchy itself. At his death he was owed nearly £5,000 – the equivalent of more than £2 million today – largely by Henry II who, it seemed, had failed to repay anything. Cade was one of the most prominent loan sharks of his age, and what is clear from his dealings is that lending, whether at interest or just to clinch an exchange, was an essential, everyday part of life in the medieval age.

The feudal, supposedly 'cashless' way of life was changing. The rates of return on land, tenancies, crops and the like were too irregular, and increasingly, agrarian lords and land-owning monasteries were opting for advances offered by increasingly canny merchants to see them through the year.

Three years before Cade's death, the Church's prohibition on usury at the Council of Tours in 1163 made it impossible for Christian financiers to lend money at interest. Cade's day was momentarily over. For the next 130 years, the Jews were to step into his shoes.

◆

Aaron of Lincoln, 1125–1186 *Financier*

C hannelled into moneylending because they were not supposed to own land or peddle any trade other than medicine, the Jewish community in England, which numbered about 5,000, had become the richest in Europe by the end of the 12th century. One of the wealthiest was Aaron of Lincoln, who built up a web of banking throughout England from his base in Lincoln.

As well as the usual propping up of the throne through finance, Lincoln very cleverly made a point of lending money for the building of abbeys and monasteries – including the Abbey of St Albans, Lincoln Minster, Peterborough Abbey and a healthy slew of nine Cistercian monasteries – in an early version of superb public relations.

In 1186, when he died, Lincoln was the second richest man in England (after the king) and was owed money by a mix of 430 people that spanned all social divides. At this point, Henry II must have rubbed his hands together in glee because the estate of the Jewish usurer, all of Lincoln's legacy, now reverted to the Crown, giving the king a sudden and very welcome spike in his balance sheet.

Lincoln's cash alone was enough to fill a ship and single-handedly finance Henry's military campaign against King Philip Augustus in France. Lincoln must have chuckled from the grave when said ship went down on the voyage over to France, sinking between Shoreham and Dieppe. But that was just the cash – so extensive were Lincoln's IOUs, so large the amount owed to him, that a separate wing of the Exchequer was created just to manage and chase the debtors. It was called 'Aaron's Exchequer'.

Lincoln's death also had a more sinister legacy. His wealth, and that of the Jewish community in general, had aroused Henry II's greed, leading him to tax the Jews in an even more debilitating way than his predecessors. In 1186, when Henry was looking for crusade funding, he demanded no less than a quarter of Jewish chattels, an amount that was expected to match the tithe extracted from the whole of the rest of the country.

This extraordinary extortion, then copied by Henry's descendants over the next century, eventually resulted in the expulsion of Jews from England under Edward I, 100 years after Henry's first heinous demand. So taxed-out by 1290 that they were no longer useful to him, and no longer allowed to lend money with interest as usurers, the king solved the problem of what to do with the Jews by simply throwing between 4,000 and 16,000 of them out. There wasn't to be another Jewish community in England until 1655.

◆

Hubert Walter, c. 1140–1205 *Chancellor*

An early beneficiary of nepotism – as a lowly clerk he rose under the eye of his uncle Ranulf de Glanville, Henry II's great justiciar – Hubert Walter went on to become the most powerful man in England.

He was an ingenious and industrious public servant who ruled the country almost single-handedly while Richard I was away on campaign. He also went on to become King John's chancellor. His stranglehold over both the Church and the state was to be unmatched until Cardinal Thomas Wolseley appeared some 400 years later.

The secret of Walter's success lay in the wide range of his talents and experience as a negotiator, judge, royal secretary and even military campaign-leader who prevented the Third Crusade from failing completely. His determination was legendary and he ignored the hatred and scorn of the monks of Canterbury when he became their archbishop, but, nevertheless, still secured for them lasting rights and advantages such as the resurrection of the ancient privilege of coining money at Canterbury.

In the meantime, he presided over one of England's most fruitful periods of administrative development, which saw the first attempt to tax revenue for secular purposes, the extraordinary quarter-levy for Richard I's ransom, the first general assize for weights and measures and the streamlining of feudal military service.

Such was his power and gravitas that, when he crowned King John in 1199, he was able to lay peculiar emphasis on the old English right to elect the Crown, knowing that he was one of the few men who could keep John the budding autocrat under control. Unfortunately, in 1204, even Walter's stated disapproval wasn't enough to stop the king from embarking on an ill-managed attempt to stem the loss of his French dominions, culminating in the final ceding of Normandy.

The Chancellor was sacked for his stand against the campaign, dying two months later of a fever 'and a carbuncle'.

◆

Henry Bracton, d. 1268 *Judge*

It was during Henry Bracton's life that the king's council diverged from the judiciary, making Bracton (or, to give him his proper name, Henry of Bratton, in Devon) one of the first of the new class of professional judges. A lifelong career in law equipped him well for his crowning achievement, a legacy that was to be untouched for 500 years. This was his long treatise *On the Laws & Customs of England*, a work so stuffed with case histories (2,000 of them) and an exploration so detailed and comprehensive that nothing else written in the Middle Ages can compare to it. Not until William Blackstone, and his famous *Commentaries on the Laws of England* (1769), would anyone even attempt to better Bracton.

◆

Sir Ralph Hengham, d. 1311 *Lord Chief Justice*

Sir Ralph Hengham's claim to fame that, despite his status as lord chief justice, he was imprisoned and fined the unlikely sum of 7,000 marks in 1290, is most likely an exaggeration (the amount has since been estimated at closer to 800 marks). The punishment seems all the more unfair given that Hengham was a faithful servant to Edward I, responsible for many of the reforms and statutes that have given this monarch his reputation as 'the English Justinian'. But a look at the timing betrays just how Hengham was a victim of Edward's need for money to fund his wars.

In 1275, the king had given the Jews of England 15 years to stop being usurers and become merchants or artisans, but had not stopped taxing them exhaustively. In 1290, after Edward returned from the Gascony battlefields, he expelled the Jewish community as being drained dry and of no use to him any more. He made Hengham and Chancellor Burnell the scapegoats for this decision, dismissing them both and silencing the former with imprisonment and bankruptcy. Hengham's crime? That he reduced the fine of a poor man, from 13 shillings (£236 today) to six shillings (£109). Hengham's own disproportionate fine was used to erect a tower in Westminster, supposedly with a clock and a bell, to remind judges of his crime. Since then, a clock tower has always stood there. Today we refer to it as Big Ben. It is said that Hengham's ghost haunts the Upper Chamber of the Houses of Parliament, still searching for the justice that eluded him in his life.

◆

Sir William de la Pole (the Younger), d. 1366   *Merchant*

As a study in increasing prosperity, the De la Pole family were top of the class in the 14th century. They came from humble roots as Welsh farmers called 'Ap Gwenwynwyn' but changed their name to 'De la Pole' and moved to Kingston-upon-Hull to set up as merchants.

The older William de la Pole had married a local fish-trade heiress with the unforgettable name of Elena Rotenheryng and had amassed enough wealth to launch the successful partnership of his two sons, Richard and William, as wool and wine merchants. William rose to become the richest English merchant of his era and, as one historian put it, 'the first to rival the Italians as a royal banker'. Even tying their wagons to the stars of Queen Isabella and Roger Mortimer – the two brothers lent them vast sums of money in 1327 alone – did not mean that the De la Poles crashed at the end of the queen's dictatorship; they were simply too rich for Edward III to drop them.

William continued as the king's financier and, in 1339, was appointed second baron of the exchequer, the year that he lent the king an unprecedented £110,000 (more than £45 million in today's money), and, in being raised to the House of Lords, was the first merchant to do so. Late in life, when he married a knight's daughter, and later married off his daughters to high-ranking aristocrats, William's social climbing was right on track. Occasionally, he got too big for his boots – fighting off convictions in 1340 and 1353 – but each time he escaped ruin to come back stronger.

By the end of his life, William had launched his family into high society, only for a later William de la Pole (see Chapter II) to bring it all crashing down again a century or so later.

◆

Nicholas Brembre, d. 1388   *Merchant*

The power of the merchant in the 1380s was not always accompanied by peaceful prosperity. Clashes between those in guilds and those selling goods without a guild licence often led to street-fighting. Even against such a backdrop, grocer Nicholas Brembre stood out for his ruthlessness in influencing the politics of London trade.

Brembre's secret weapon, through his loans to the Crown, was his cultivation of friends in high places and the support of King Richard II. Brembre left his grocer days behind in 1377 and was appointed Lord Mayor of London. He was one of two collectors of customs for the Port of London for many years and, in 1381, was knighted. However, by 1387, after a bruising period back as mayor, in which he was accused of beheading a cordwainer without trial and of securing elections by violence, he had lined up too many enemies and, as Richard's sun waned, was too tightly linked with the king. Brembre was charged with taking 22 prisoners (an exaggeration) out of Newgate and beheading them without trial; his plea, as a knight, for trial by battle, was rejected. He was beheaded on 20 February 1388.

◆

Sir Peter de la Mare, d. circa 1388 *Speaker*

When a humble knight and toll collector from Hereford stood up to address what is now known as the 'Good Parliament' of 1376, he became the first known Speaker of the House of Commons. Peter de la Mare was also unexpectedly eloquent and extraordinarily daring, attacking the perceived corruption of the court, bewailing England's recent military failures, condemning the crippling level of taxation being poured into the war and concluding with the brave words: 'And so, the common people are demanding a statement of accounts from those who received the money, for it is not credible that the king should need such an infinitely large sum if his ministers were loyal.' The king's ministers – first and foremost, John of Gaunt – were speechless at such observations. 'What are these degenerate knights of tallow undertaking?' Gaunt was heard to say. 'Do they think they are kings or princes of this land? I will terrify them with such severity, that neither they nor anybody like them will dare in future to challenge my majesty.'

Despite having such a formidable enemy – and being imprisoned briefly in 1376 – De la Mare was compensated for his treatment and went on to serve in several parliaments in the 1380s. Gone were the days when such minor figures could be stamped underfoot; coming were the days where the House of Commons actually had some sort of influence.

◆

William Wykeham, 1324–1404 *Bishop and civil servant*

Patron of education and architect William Wykeham was also the most blatant pluralist of his time. In four years alone, between 1357 and 1361, he had rectories, prebends, canonries, a deaconry and an archdeaconry granted to him, with all the beneficial incomes that those conveyed, making him one of the richest men in England. He was, as one historian commented, 'the ultimate civil servant bishop'.

That said, however, he owed it all to one man: the king. Despite Wykeham's relative lack of education, let alone vocation, Edward III had favoured him ever since his days as the royal clerk of the works, in charge of Edward's beloved buildings, and by the 1360s, relied on him entirely. It was said that Wykeham 'reigned in England, and without him nothing was done'. In the 1370s, there were a few hiccups in his secular career, but nearly 30 years after he first held the post of chancellor, he was re-appointed between 1389 and 1391. It could be said he had a political career of extraordinary length and survival.

Wykeham died at the age of 80, leaving his enormous wealth to his colleges, a nephew and the bulk to charity. He also left behind him a spiritual legacy of education that was imitated down through the centuries, as well as Winchester Cathedral, which began to change from the Norman to the airy splendours of the Perpendicular style under Wykeham's eye.

Richard Whittington, c. 1350–1423   *Merchant*

C all this merchant and politician 'Dick' and give him a cat and suddenly everybody will know who he is. Pantomime halls across the country have thrilled to the slap of hands on to principal boys' thighs as this feel-good tale of a humble lad heading to the capital to seek his fortune unfolds. Of course, the truth is more prosaic and the image of a young man with his belongings tied into a handkerchief on a stick doesn't square with the real Richard Whittington's birth as the younger son of an affluent family in Gloucestershire, sent to learn the mercer trade.

Nevertheless, Whittington did come to London to seek and make his fortune. He quickly became a successful trader in silks, velvets and wool cloth, then branched out into moneylending from 1388. In 1397, as Richard II's appointee to London's vacant mayoral post, Whittington persuaded the king to let the city buy back its old liberties for the sum of £10,000 (more than £3.5 million in today's money); so grateful were the citizens of London that he was elected as mayor by them as well – an unusually consensual conclusion borne out by his re-election three further times.

While amassing great wealth – which, childless, he left to benefit the city in his will – Whittington was also famous for his simple lifestyle and commitment to good works. These included a ward for unmarried mothers at St Thomas's Hospital, sewerage systems around Billingsgate and Cripplegate, the first public drinking fountains, and one of London's first 'official' public lavatories that was washed out by the River Thames at high tide.

The appearance of Whittington's cat (in the story, Dick's cat is sold to the rat-infested Emperor of China, which then makes his fortune) came about nearly 200 years after Whittington's death, from a well-circulated early engraving of the mayor, in which his hand rested upon a cat. Closer examination revealed that the oddly-curled cat was actually a skull, a popular pose in portraits then . So there is, in fact, no evidence that Whittington even owned a cat.

◆

John Howard, 1430–1485 *Duke of Norfolk*

Born into minor gentry, John Howard became the 15th century's equivalent of a self-made man. He became vastly rich and the third person to resurrect the Duchy of Norfolk, being created Duke of Norfolk in 1483. He became Sheriff of Norfolk and Suffolk, treasurer of the Royal Household, envoy to France and, finally, lord admiral of all England, Ireland and Aquitaine.

At Edward IV's funeral in 1483, he alone carried the king's banner, then swiftly attached himself to Richard III. Known as Jack or Jock, Howard was famously warned the night before the Battle of Bosworth that this might not have been such a good move, given that Richard had been double-crossed, finding the following note: 'Jockey of Norfolk, be not too bold, For Dickon, thy Master, is bought and sold.' However, the warning was to no avail. Howard was killed on the field and was attainted (his lineage slandered) at Henry VII's first parliament.

No one could have predicted that half a century later, his granddaughters, Anne Boleyn and Catherine Howard, would become, respectively, the second and fifth wives of King Henry VIII.

CHAPTER VIII

◆

ROGUES, REBELS & RIOTERS

Hereward the Wake, active between 1060–1070   *Legendary rebel*

A swamp-based bandit banished by Edward the Confessor for being a troublemaker, or mythical hero leading popular opposition to William the Conqueror? Hereward the Wake is one of our more romantic rebels, but he is shrouded in mystery and is also a somewhat unlikely legend. In the *Gesta Herewardi*, written about 100 years after Hereward was alive, there are tales which wax lyrical about the grey wolf that guides his companions through the marshlands surrounding Ely, while will-o'-the-wisp lights flicker around their spear tips. Accounts of his life start prosaically enough.

He was believed to be the son of an Anglo-Saxon lord, Leofric. He was thought to be a mercenary in Europe at the time of the conquest and to have returned in 1070, joining up with an army supplied by the Danish ruler Sweith Estrithson, to establish a base of resistance on the Isle of Ely, home to a monastery. The story goes that the Normans made a full-blown attack on the island, aided by a mile-long timber causeway, which sank under the weight of horses, men and armour. Then a cunning Norman knight, Belsar, bribed the island monks to show them a safe path through the swamps surrounding Ely. This allowed them to sneak up on Hereward's force and take them unawares. In the ensuing fracas, Hereward escaped with some of his men into the fenland, disappearing from record. Some say he was reconciled with William, even fighting for him in France, before being killed by jealous Norman knights. Some say he continued his resistance as an underground hero, while others say the reality is more squalid. They argue it was all about a squabble over land rights and estates, to which he then retired.

Meanwhile, his exploits managed to capture the popular imagination: ballads, dances and chronicles about a quick-witted guerilla fighter, nicknamed 'the Wake' for his heroic watchfulness led to modern-day novels, cartoons, TV series and even a mention in a Pink Floyd track called 'Let There Be More Light'.

William Longbeard, d. 1196   *Social agitator*

ocial agitator and self-proclaimed 'saviour of the poor', William Longbeard had been part of the establishment of the City of London, before placing himself at the head of an uprising by the unenfranchised townsmen against the wealthier burgesses, merchant guilds and aldermen. His defiance and eloquence earned him widespread popularity, but he was unable to win over the court of Richard I, who needed the moneyed classes on its side to pay for Richard's overseas campaigns. The justiciar, Archbishop Hubert Walter, issued a demand for his arrest. Longbeard felled the first soldier that came at him with an axe and fled to the tower of St Mary-le-Bow. Despite his vestments, the archbishop denied Longbeard his sanctuary by setting fire to the tower and smoking him out.

When Longbeard was hanged at Smithfield, there was a mad rush for his corpse – part of the belief in the medieval age that the bodies of the hanged were efficacious in the healing of disease – with people fighting over the hairs on his head (against evil spirits) or even a shred from his clothes (protection from aches and pains). Stranger still, superstitious women came from all over the Home Counties to collect the mould at the foot of his gallows, conferring upon Longbeard more importance in death than he had really earned in life.

◆

Robin Hood, most likely active c. 1200   *Legendary folk hero*

his merry man is the archetypal folk hero: a kindly, pious, generous and swashbuckling outlaw who embodied the struggle between the dastardly Norman-French ruling elite and the honest, hard-working

English. It seems churlish to try to pin him down, work out who he is and separate the myth from the reality, but doing this has been the game of historians throughout the centuries.

Was he Robin of Locksley, a nobleman who turns to heroic crime as revenge after coming back from the crusades to find corrupt local officials, embodied by the villainous Sheriff of Nottingham, have taken his lands away? Or, is he an earlier outlaw, an Anglo-Saxon putting up resistance to the depredations of the ruling Normans? Did he operate out of Sherwood Forest in Nottinghamshire, according to modern storytellers, or did he – as was more likely – actually hail from Barnsdale Forest in West Yorkshire, with its Robin Hood's Well, string of Robin Hood pubs and now the Robin Hood Doncaster Sheffield Airport?

What is clear, however, is that the idea of merry men in green, living a bucolic existence up a tree and robbing from the rich to give to the poor is a *post-hoc* invention – dating from the 15th and 16th centuries and embroidered right up to the present day by no less than 44 movies – starring the likes of Errol Flynn and Kevin Costner – and numerous television series, the latest of which made its debut in 2006 with handsome newcomer Jonas Armstrong in the title role of the 13-episode BBC production.

The original ballads and chronicles give a far grittier picture. It's more of the violent outlaw and less of the social justice programme. The enemies are there – a corrupt sheriff, an evil bounty hunter called Guy of Gisborne and a scheming churchman whom Robin tricks and humiliates – but there is no mention of him giving money to the poor, nor of the idea that he was a rebel fighting against the depredations of Prince John, determined to hold the fort until good King Richard came back from the crusades. Whatever the truth behind Robin Hood, he joins the likes of Hereward the Wake in what was to become a peculiarly English love for the plucky resistance hero taking on the elite in the name of everyman. Historical detail be damned!

Simon de Montfort, 1208–1265   *Rebel*

erhaps the best-known rebel of the Middle Ages, it is from Simon de Montfort that the modern idea of a democratically representative parliament first developed. He arrived at the English court in 1231, seeking to clear a path to inheriting some English estates in Leicester, and soon became one of the king's favourites.

Love led him into trouble in 1238 in the curvaceous form of Henry III's widowed sister Eleanor – although only 16 when her first husband had died, she had sworn a vow of chastity. It was only after his seduction of her and their secret wedding that De Montfort received permission from the king. With that achieved, all should have ended well, but a mixture of De Montfort's debts and his habit of using his royal connections as surety led to an enmity between the once-close brothers-in-law.

By 1258, at the 'Mad Parliament' of Oxford, 42 years into Henry's reign, De Montfort was merely one of a group of disaffected barons who'd had enough of the king's descent into incompetency. They thought him blind to his country's troubles and were angered by his disregard for the principles of the Magna Carta, signed only 43 years before.

Having agreed to the 'provisions' that were the updated version of the Great Charter, Henry then went on to ignore them. For De Montfort, this was when the die was cast. He wanted to force the king to govern more constitutionally. This led to full-blown rebellion in 1263, to the easily-won Battle of Lewes in 1264 (when he captured the king and Prince Edward) and, for the next 18 months, a regime under which he single-handedly governed the country.

Having written a new constitution for England, called the 'Mise of Lewes', for 'De Montfort's Parliament' of 1265, De Montfort asked all the counties and selected boroughs to send in elected representatives, even if they were commoners. This was unheard of. The barons who had earlier supported him started to get cold feet. The collapse of the regime came quickly. Prince Edward escaped custody and raised an army from an array of De Montfort's enemies.

In August 1265, Edward dealt De Montfort a crushing blow on the slopes of the River Avon at Evesham. After just two hours the battle was over. De Montfort was dead, his body dismembered and its parts sent around England, and Henry's long reign limped to a sordid, shabby close.

◆

Roger Mortimer, 1287–1330 *Baron and royal favourite*

For romance, skullduggery, treachery and bravado, it would be hard to beat the story of Roger Mortimer. In just nine years this former courtier and Marcher baron had run the gamut, from soldier in the Scottish wars to leader of an uprising by barons against the hated royal favourites, the Despensers; to Tower of London escapee; to lover of his monarch's wife, Queen Isabella; to probable murderer of her husband, Edward II; to virtual dictator of England; to convicted traitor and scapegoat, sentenced to hang by his mistress's son, Edward III.

Along the way he made many enemies, including former allies like the Earl of Lancaster. Even his son, Geoffrey, mocked his ambition, calling him 'the king of folly' for claiming descent from King Arthur, while others decried his opportunism in Wales (where he enriched himself with a flagrant disrespect for any law).

Lately, the blame laid at the feet of Mortimer for the murder of Edward II has come under the microscope. Historians are investigating the idea that Edward was not murdered, but was spirited away. The theory being that his death was concocted for political purposes and that he was, in fact, still alive in 1330. Should the case be proved, Mortimer would be placed firmly in the clear in this one instance.

◆

Adam the Leper, c. 1320–1360 *Gang leader*

𝕬 dam the Leper was no political rebel, he was more a good old-fashioned villain, who made the usual cut-throats and petty thieves of the Middle Ages look like small fry indeed.

Not content with simple banditry, kidnapping and the usual moneyspinners of the age, Adam and his desperately-feared gang would terrorise entire neighbourhoods. They would time their attacks very carefully; when fairs were in town and they could assume that townsfolk were out and about, the gang would sweep down, rob the houses, then set fire to them. No one ever pursued them because they were too busy coping with the fires.

Adam started thinking big in 1347. He took on the town of Bristol, robbing a trader of jewellery intended for the queen and plundering ships in the harbour, some of which belonged to Edward III. Enough was enough, thought the king, and sent the full force of the law to capture Adam – but to no avail. When Adam was arraigned and tried in Winchester, his gang waited outside and attacked everyone who came in or out. The authorities decided to drop their action. Adam got away for more crime-filled days, but never again attempted to steal from the Crown.

◆

Wat Tyler, d. 1381 *Revolt leader*

I t is highly likely that Wat Tyler did not choose to lead the Peasants'
Revolt of 1381, but had that double-edged greatness thrust upon him
– for all of a week – following his own impetuous reaction to the callousness
of the poll tax collectors. The story goes that a taxman tried to determine
whether Kentishman Tyler's daughter was of taxable age (15) by ripping her
clothes off and feeling for himself. Hearing the screams of both wife and
daughter, Tyler came running, only to smash in the head of the taxman with
a hammer, whereupon his neighbours and others, rippling out all across the
county, were inspired to rise up in protest.

The fixed (per head) levy was the final straw after the horrendous
decades following the Black Death of 1348. As much as half the country's
population had died in the plague; the feudal lords, short of tenants, were
dogged in trying to crack down on the movements and wages of those who
were left. Even those who had survived lived no better than animals.
Added to this were the disastrous campaigns in France which led, in
particular, to Kent's coast being harried and raided. Soon, a mob of around
100,000 were marching on London, breaking open every prison on the
way but still maintaining discipline so that their agenda of social change
would remain unsullied.

On 14 June 1381, Richard II, then only 14 years of age, rode out to meet
the rebels at Mile End, offering a friendly ear to their grievances,
whereupon Tyler and the rebels thought they had succeeded. Flushed with
victory, the discipline of the peasants dissolved; they rampaged through the
city, taking over the Tower of London and beheading most senior officials
they came across, including the Archbishop of Canterbury. The next day,
according to chroniclers, saw Tyler sauntering up for another parley with
the young monarch at Smithfield, demanding a drink of water and
then spitting it out 'in an uncouth manner'. His arrogance enraged the

Mayor of London. In the ensuing fight Tyler was stabbed to death. This could have been the flashpoint for the peasants massed behind, but Richard kept a cool head, riding out to the mob and crying out: 'Sirs, will you shoot your king? I will be your chief and captain, you shall have from me all that you seek!'

This was the chivalric pinnacle of Richard's reign. The following weeks saw the young king renege on his promises of reform and pardon. He hanged 1,500 rebels and revoked all measures towards the enfranchisement of peasants. It was just the start of things to come in the badly-judged reign that followed.

◆

John Ball, d. 1381 *Revoltist*

J ohn Ball was the 'mad priest' (as a chronicler described him) that gave the Peasants' Revolt its moral and spiritual authority. Unlike Wat Tyler, Ball was already well known as a denouncer of clerical abuses and a preacher of social equality in his home town of York and his later base of Essex, long before the events of 1381. By 1364 he had been excommunicated and, in 1366, all persons were forbidden to hear him preach. But that didn't stop him. Churches, churchyards, markets and sundry other 'profance places' were disrupted by his diatribes, which encouraged the non-payment of tithes and questioned the Church's policy of celibacy.

While serving the last of his many jail sentences, this time at Maidstone in Kent, Ball was freed by a Kentish mob intent on having its manifesto heard in London. Armed with the inspiration of William Langland and his poem 'Piers Plowman', and possessing a reputedly extraordinary gift of the gab, Ball wowed the massed rebels at Blackheath with his crowd-pleasing talk. He waxed lyrical about bringing down lords, lawyers, bishops and archbishops and sharing out their property. Flushed with righteousness, the mob swept on into London, singling out the Bishop of London and the king's treasurer for particular venom. They were taken from a captured Tower of London and beheaded. The same fate also awaited Ball. When Tyler was murdered and the Peasants' Revolt fell apart, Ball fled to the Midlands, but was captured in Coventry. He was hanged, drawn, quartered and beheaded in St Albans in front of the king himself, a mere month after he and his fellow rebels had been granted pardons.

◆

Sir Henry Percy, 1364–1403 *Harry Hotspur*

ith his noble lineage, reputation as a warrior and the key part he played in putting Henry IV on the throne, 'Harry Hotspur' should not be included in this chapter. But, because of the role he played in the brutal rebellion which also ended his life, he is eligible. As one biographer said: 'Hotspur was to become living testament to his family's impetuous need to prove itself in a world of political and chivalric extremes.'

Coming from one of the most powerful families of the north, eldest son of the first Percy Earl of Northumberland, Sir Henry Percy earned his 'Hotspur' nickname for his zeal in the border warfare that dominated his teenage years. He was a battle-scarred veteran of both Scottish and French struggles by the time he was 24 and had earned himself a reputation as a war hero at the battle of Otterburn in 1388. As his family's reward for being the force behind Henry Bolingbroke's successful bid for the throne in 1399,

Hotspur and his Percy kin were given both East and West Marches, the justiciar's post in North Wales and more castles than he could shake a lance at. So where did it all go wrong?

William Shakespeare, in his rousing dramatisations of the period in *Henry IV Parts I* and *II*, would have us believe that there was principle and high-mindedness involved, but the reality was a little more prosaic. Henry didn't pay Hotspur's wages, even when Hotspur continued to fight his battles for him, as at the Battle of Homildon Hill. The invading Scottish army was nearly destroyed, the English loss was said to have been five men, and Hotspur had a valuable hostage as his personal prisoner. Both Hotspur and Henry IV fancied using the hostage, Douglas, as a bargaining chip. The dispute over who 'owned' him flared up into face-to-face conflict, during which Henry called Hotspur a traitor, struck him on the face and drew his sword. Hotspur reputedly answered with: 'Not here, but on the field.'

Some say that Hotspur was dead even before battle was joined, hit by an arrow in the mouth and killed instantly. Initially, Henry IV was said to have wept when his old friend's body was brought to him for burial, but he soon hardened his heart, forbade its interment and had it quartered – the four parts were sent around England as an example of what happened to traitors. Hotspur's head was stuck on a pole at the gates of York.

◆

Sir John Oldcastle, d. 1417   *Friend to Henry V turned rebel*

Held by some historians to be the original inspiration for William Shakespeare's character Falstaff, Sir John Oldcastle was the old friend, and fellow Welsh campaigner, of Henry V; he later turned to rebellion through his Lollard religious tendencies. At the time it was estimated that John Wycliffe had an incredible 400,000 followers – nearly half the adult males of all classes – all wishing for a return to simpler, more scriptural, less corrupt religion. Having been convicted of Lollard heresies in 1413, after one of his religious texts had been discovered in a London bookshop, Oldcastle's execution had been deferred by the influence of his old friend, the king, into a respite of 40 days.

He then escaped from the Tower of London and put himself at the heart of a directed Lollard conspiracy, an uprising that was coupled with a plot to kidnap the king and his brothers while they were at a Twelfth Night Mumming performance. Henry found out his intention, the attempt failed and Oldcastle fled. His crime was too great this time around, and the king's protection, quite understandably, fell away.

When Oldcastle was finally tracked down two years later, he was brought, wounded, to be hanged over a slow fire.

◆

Owain Glyndwr, 1359–c. 1416 *Welsh rebel*

wain Glyndwr, sometimes anglicised to Owen Glendower, was both the last Prince of Wales and the last hope for Wales; he was the instigator of a final doomed rebellion against the English, and one of the many thorns in the side of Henry IV. After Richard II's reign, whose final days had seen a loosening of the traditional Marcher Lords' grip on the region, allowing Welshmen more opportunities, Henry's accession threatened a return to the bad old days. A land dispute between 50-year-old Glyndwr and one of the favourites of the new ruler provided the spark for an uprising in 1400, which quickly swept through northern and central Wales. The rebels, made up of Glyndwr's men and those who came to join him, called themselves 'Plant Owain', which, loosely translated, means the 'Children of Owen'. In 1402, the sighting of a great comet in the sky was hailed by Glyndwr's supporters as a sign of victory and, by the following year, there was reason for jubilation as the revolt gained ground. With the French joining in to help the Welsh, even the great castles of Carmarthen, Abergavenny, Harlech and Aberystwyth fell, with Caernarfon almost falling to Glyndwr's men.

This was to prove a campaign of astonishing brutality on both sides, with hardly a parish or family in Wales remaining unaffected. But early Welsh success was countered when Prince Harry cleverly blockaded Welsh efforts to get either food supplies or weapons. In 1409, the last stand of Glyndwr and his family at Harlech collapsed. Glyndwr escaped but was a hunted man, with nothing seen of him after 1412.

There was the odd spurt of resistance in the following years, but Henry V placated most rebels with pardons and made peace with the new order. Bearing remarkable similarities to the English tale of King Arthur, Welsh legend states that when Wales is threatened again, Glyndwr will rise from his secret place to save his people.

◆

Jack Cade, d. 1450 *Irish rebel*

Whether a deliberate act or just an accident of history, so much of Jack Cade is shrouded in mystery. His origins, his name, even the place of his death are unknown. Was he an Irishman who had settled in

Sussex, only to flee after killing a woman? Or a disgraced physician who had to escape a messy scandal involving a patient's death? Was he a former military captain under the King of France? Who was Jack Cade, the name by which he led? John Mortimer, the name by which he was pardoned? John Amend-All, the name by which he wooed his followers? All we know is that he appeared out of nowhere to become the charismatic leader of the 1450 Cade Rebellion; a swashbuckler resplendent in expensive armour and impressive sword, clever enough to present the rebels' grievances in different manifestos, according to their audience.

This uprising was by no means another Peasants' Revolt, but a much wider social gathering. Landowners, knights, lesser gentry, tradesmen and even respectable churchmen mixed in with peasants, and they were all protesting against rumours of Kent being turned into a royal forest, as well as the breakdown of law, order and integrity in the disintegrating decades leading up to the Wars of the Roses. Forced labour, corrupt courts, the seizure of land by greedy aristocrats, the loss of English dominions in France and the punishing taxation of a beleaguered Crown were the issues at the forefront of the uprising, but Cade and his band of followers were not pushing for a wider social agenda, they were merely pleading for a 'fix it', not a 'change it', solution.

Having beaten an initial royal force at Sevenoaks, they stormed a London that had been abandoned by the king, only just failing to take the Tower of London. Henry VI was forced to negotiate through officials brandishing nearly 2,000 pardons and promising Cade that his list of demands would go right to the top. Faced with what looked like success, most rebels melted away back to Kent; however, all their grievances were roundly ignored and, under the pretext that Jack Cade and some followers had continued to bear arms after the pardon, they were hunted down and executed by the king's men.

In Cade's case, he was cornered and mortally wounded by the new Sheriff of Kent – it was thought – in a hamlet in Sussex then re-named Cade Street.

Recently, though, even this theory has been questioned, with the conclusion that he was actually more likely to have met his doom in Hothfield, Kent, in July 1450.

◆

Perkin Warbeck, 1474–1499 *Irish fraudster*

When the good burghers of Cork saw a young gentleman in 1491, walking the streets of the city, proud in the finest clothes, they decided he must be of royal birth and declared he was Richard, the younger brother of Edward V, both of whom had disappeared eight years before in the Tower of London. And so began one of the most bizarre frauds ever. The young man in question was called Perkin Warbeck and he was from Tournai in Flanders. Warbeck was doing what many students dressed in massive billboards do nowadays when he was spotted, he was being a walking advertisement for his master, a silk merchant. When the local earls of Desmond and Kildare got wind of this they, and then some more senior intriguers, encouraged the illusion that he was one of the princes who had been feared murdered in 1483.

By 1492 Warbeck had become sufficiently notorious to attract the attention of the higher echelons in both France and England. He visited Edward IV's sister Margaret in Flanders, was treated as the lawful ruler in Vienna and, in July 1495, tried to invade England before landing in Ireland. A feeble attack on Waterford left him fleeing to Scotland where King James IV treated him kindly and arranged a good marriage for him. In 1497, he was on his way again, landing in Cornwall and joining up with a mob of already disaffected peasants to form an army of revolt. He marched on Exeter but, as the royal troops hove into view, he showed his less-than-royal courage and bolted, finally surrendering in September 1497.

His wife was kindly treated and taken into the household of Henry VII's wife Elizabeth, but Warbeck himself was hanged in November 1499, having confessed publicly that he was a fraudster.

CHAPTER IX

FORMIDABLE LADIES

Matilda, 1101–1167   *Empress and queen*

Often called Maud to differentiate her from the many other Matildas of her era, Matilda was the daughter and dispossessed heir of Henry I. She was the wife of, first, Holy Roman Emperor Henry V (hence the 'Empress' title) and then, less successfully, Geoffrey of Anjou, 11 years her junior, and the originator of the family nickname, Plantagenet, which comes from the broom flower (*planta genista* or *plant á genet*) that was his emblem. With Anjou, Matilda became the parent of another Henry – Henry II.

She was also, if only for a brief moment, the first-ever female English monarch. When her father's wish to put her on the throne was stymied by her cousin Stephen's usurpation, plunging the country into the chaos referred to as 'the anarchy', Matilda also revealed herself to be the first royal escapologist. Backed into a corner in early 1141, she escaped from Devizes by disguising herself as a corpse and being carried out for burial. Later, having defeated Stephen and ruling for a few tense, unpopular months as the 'Lady of the English', her rival escaped and besieged her at Oxford in 1142. Undaunted, Matilda escaped by fleeing across the snow-covered landscape, wearing an all-white fur cape as camouflage. Once 'the anarchy' was resolved and her son, Henry II, was safely on the throne, Matilda retired to her own court in Normandy.

Although reputedly proud and haughty, Matilda's epitaph makes her out to be humble indeed. It says: 'Here lies the daughter, wife and mother of Henry.' It was to be another 300 years before there would be another Queen of England – Henry VIII's hated daughter, Mary I.

◆

Eleanor of Aquitaine, 1122–1204   *Wife of two monarchs*

ne of the wealthiest and most powerful women of the Middle Ages, Eleanor of Aquitaine led a life that would put modern-day soap opera divas to shame. The red-haired, brown-eyed, famously intelligent and legendarily beautiful Eleanor was the apple of her father William X's eye and was given the best possible education in one of Europe's most sophisticated courts, home to poets and troubadours and the fount of the tradition of courtly love. By the time she reached 25, she had been orphaned, had been married to Louis VII of France in an arranged match for nearly a decade and had even been on crusade along with 300 of her ladies-in-waiting, not as camp-followers, but dressed reputedly as Amazons, in armour, carrying lances and riding white horses.

Eleanor's crusading and her trail of lovers across the Mediterranean marked the death-knell of her marriage to the dry-as-dust Louis VII, even though he adored her. A mere six weeks after the annulment of that particular union, Eleanor married the dashing Count of Anjou and Duke of Normandy, who, at 19, was 11 years her junior. The duke would eventually become her second monarch husband when he became Henry II, ruler of England, in 1154.

The new couple were extraordinarily powerful with their joint holdings of England, Normandy, Anjou, Poitiers and Aquitaine, but Eleanor had met her match this time around. She and Henry had five sons and three daughters over the next 13 years, but the lows were as dramatic as the highs, and Eleanor stormed off to Poitiers and Aquitaine in 1168 to set up an independent court in disgust at Henry's involvement with Thomas Becket's murder in 1170. This culminated in the Great Revolt of 1173 when she sided with not only her ex-husband Louis VII of France against Henry, but also with their three elder sons, Henry the Young King, Geoffrey and Richard.

As a result, Eleanor was dragged back to England and, for the next 15 years, was imprisoned in a series of castles and palaces around England and France.

Her son Richard I's first act on his accession to the throne in 1189, was to order her release. For the following 15 years Eleanor returned to the mainstream of court life. She ran England as Richard's regent while he was off crusading and personally negotiated his ransom and went to release him from his captivity in Germany. Tireless in her efforts to cement her family's alliances throughout Europe, Eleanor also picked out Richard's wife Berengaria and escorted her to Sicily to meet her new husband. She also oversaw the match between her 13-year-old granddaughter, Blanche of Castile, and Louis VIII of France.

She died at the ripe old age of 82 and was buried at Fontrevault, a peaceful Angevin abbey, next to Henry II. Eleanor had outlived all of her children except John and her daughter Leonora, and left a legacy that embraced Bordeaux wine, 'courtly love' poetry and even the introduction of opium from the Middle East into Europe.

◆

Isabella of Angoulême, 1187–1246 *Queen to King John*

Was it a disastrous strategic calculation or just uncontrollable sexual desire that led King John to divorce his wife of many years, and marry 12-year-old Isabella of Angoulême? Since it's hard to see why anyone would think that stealing the fiancée of one of the most powerful Lords of Poitou, Hugh de Lusignan, would be a wise move we can generally assume the latter.

During Christmas 1202, and despite perilous military pressure on his Norman frontier, John and Isabella were recorded as preferring to stay in bed together, enjoying sumptuous feasts and laughing off courtiers who dared approach with news from his forces. Despite the fact that Isabella bore John five children, it was still not a successful marriage. She was too fiery and, after she inherited Angoulême, was too independent. Also, John was suspicious of her fidelity, reputedly putting her under house arrest at Gloucester in December 1214. Such flightiness was borne out in the eyes of contemporaries when, following John's death and a short period putting in place the regency of her son Henry III, Isabella scooted back to Angoulême to marry Hugh de Lusignan, not her original fiancé, but his son, and the ex-fiancé of her own daughter, Joan. She was just 30 years old.

Isabella spent the last two decades of her life bearing her second husband the Poitevin sons that went on to challenge Henry III's nobles decades later and attempting to bridge the interests of her two families.

◆

Eleanor of Provence, 1223–1291   *Queen to King Henry III*

At just 12 years of age Eleanor married Henry III sight unseen in 1236, and at first was the quintessence of a respectable consort. She was famously beautiful, as pious as her husband and a devoted mother.

When her youngest child, Katherine, died aged four of a degenerative disease that had rendered her mute, both her parents were noted for their overpowering grief. But with her came a flock of 'cousins' known as the Savoyards from her native courts of Provence and Savoy, who muscled their way into court favours and patronage, much to the annoyance of the easily disgruntled barons. This is likely to have been one of the reasons for Eleanor's own unpopularity. The barons, though, had drastically underestimated Eleanor.

From being a child bride in a foreign land, she had matured into a major political player. Already trusted enough to be Henry's regent while he was away fighting in France between 1253–1254, Eleanor came into her own in her tireless fighting for Henry's corner. For example, she raised an invasion force from France to bring down Simon de Montfort's rebellion, when Henry and Prince Edward were in his custody, and put herself into the firing line to the extent where, sailing down the Thames in 1263, her barge was attacked by pro-Montfort citizens of London.

Even after Henry's death in 1272, Eleanor spent the remaining 20 years of her life as a powerful and influential dowager queen, still consulted by Edward I, her son, maintaining close links with the exchequer, chancery and justiciary, and raising several of her grandchildren.

When her grandson, Henry, died in her care in 1274 a heartbroken Eleanor retired from public life, but she did not return to her birthplace. Instead, she remained in England, entering a convent in Amesbury where she died in 1291. After her death, Eleanor was remembered as 'devout and merciful... a friend to all Englishmen and, indeed, a pillar of the realm'.

◆

Isabella of France, 1295–1358 *Queen to King Edward II*

ne of our more notorious formidable ladies, Isabella earned herself the moniker 'She-Wolf of France' for her ruthless conduct towards her husband and his kingdom, and her blatant adultery with Roger Mortimer.

Her origins, however, were impeccable. Related to four French monarchs, she had been promised as a tiny girl to Edward II, to resolve conflicts between England and France over England's French dominions. When she married handsome Edward at the beginning of his reign, she was a mere 12 years of age, already described by rapturous chroniclers as 'the beauty of beauties'. Yet even though they had four children together, Edward simply wasn't interested. He preferred his favourite, Piers Gaveston, to whom he apparently even gave her bridal jewels.

Isabella put up with years of neglect from her husband before begging Edward, when pregnant with their youngest child, to banish the latest and most rapacious of his acolytes, Hugh le Despenser the Younger. When the banished Le Despenser was recalled by the king after less than a year, it was the last straw. Isabella stormed off to France where she parleyed with her brother King Charles IV. Then, with her new lover Mortimer by her side, she went for the top prize.

In September 1326, she landed in Suffolk with an invasion force, bent on toppling her husband. Edward was apopleptic, carrying a knife in his hose with which to kill his wife and swearing that, if he had no other weapon, he would crush her with his teeth, but his threats proved empty and ineffectual.

Isabella and Mortimer swept all before them, Edward was captured and forced to abdicate in favour of his 13-year-old son, the future King Edward III. Isabella and Mortimer ran the country as if it were their own personal fiefdom during Edward III's minority but, on turning 17, the new monarch flexed his muscles, had Mortimer executed for treason and, in 1330, stormed into his mother's bedchamber at Nottingham Castle to tell her he was in charge now. Thereafter, he ensured her a very comfortable upkeep and took care to hush up references to her Mortimer affair. Given her earlier life, her decision to take the veil as a Poor Clare nun and live out her long dotage in quiet asceticism in Norfolk was even more unexpected.

Joan of Kent, 1328–1385   *The 'Fair Maid of Kent'*

When only 12 years of age, Joan of Kent – known down the ages since as the 'Fair Maid of Kent' – entered into a secret marriage with Thomas Holland, having bewitched him with her heart-shaped face, long chestnut hair, and dark, flashing eyes. But the Montague family, with whom Joan had grown up, had other plans. The following year, while Holland was overseas on military service, they forced Joan to marry their kinsman, William Montacute, Earl of Salisbury. It was during this bigamous second marriage that Joan reputedly – and inadvertently – helped to found the Order of the Garter, the story being that it was her whose 'intimate apparel' dropped to the floor, while dancing with her cousin Edward III.

Joan wasn't happy in the marriage and, when Montacute discovered that she wanted to end it, he kept her a virtual prisoner in her own home. All to no avail, however. The pope took the Hollands' side and annulled Joan's marriage to Montacute, whereupon she returned to Thomas Holland in 1349 and lived with him until his death 11 years later, bearing him four children.

Enter the third man to have been in love with her since they were children together: her cousin, Edward the Black Prince. They were married within the year, and immediately left for France where Edward took up his duties as Prince of Aquitaine and the couple had two sons, one of whom died in infancy. However, Edward's health was ravaged when he fought off the plague, and he died in 1376, a week before his 46th birthday. Joan was now a dowager, concentrating on her son, especially once he became the ruler, Richard II, at the tender age of 10.

But he was to be the cause of her death when, in 1385, he refused to lift a death sentence on her son (and his half-brother) John Holland for the manslaughter of one of the new queen's favourites. Joan pleaded for four days straight for Richard II to show mercy and died, reputedly, of a broken heart on the fifth day. Richard ended up pardoning John Holland, but it was too little, too late.

◆

Margaret of Anjou, 1429–1482   *Queen to King Henry VI*

A queen who turned out to be a more reliable figurehead on the battlefield than her own husband, Henry VI, Margaret of Anjou was one of the major Lancastrian protagonists of the Wars of the Roses. It was lucky for the Lancastrians that she was so capable. Henry's mental instability saw the emergence of the Yorkists – Richard of York was made Protector of the Realm – but Margaret wasn't going to let the monarchy go quietly. As the country degenerated into civil war, and in the ebbing and flowing of Lancastrian fortunes over the next 10 years, Margaret was an indomitable force on their side. In exile she ran a quasi-government, she forged delicate diplomatic alliances with her European relations, raised troops in France and led armies into battle.

After one defeat, the story goes that she was wandering in a Northumbrian forest and, meeting a notoriously ferocious robber, threw herself successfully on his mercy by revealing who she was. Later, such quick-wittedness led her to court Richard Neville, Earl of Warwick and 'Kingmaker', when he fell out with his former Yorkist friends. Sadly, their plan for a shared invasion went wrong. She set off too late to join her new ally; Warwick was killed by Edward IV at Barnet and Margaret led her own army into defeat at the Battle of Tewkesbury in 1471. With her son Edward killed on the battlefield, her husband put to death by Edward IV soon after and the Lancastrians in disarray, Margaret's ruthlessness crumbled, leaving her a broken woman. Captured after Tewkesbury, the queen was shuttled around various English castles until King Louis XI arranged for her release, only to abandon her to extreme poverty in Anjou until her death in 1482. It was a thankless end to a life of plotting on her husband's behalf.

◆

Margaret Paston, d. 1484 *Medieval chronicler*

The writings of Margaret Paston have bequeathed us a unique and comprehensive insight into life in the 15th century. At a time when her lawyer husband, John, was more often away than he was at home, she almost single-handedly ran their family estates, often in the face of the depredations of their enemies, the De la Poles and Norfolks, against the backdrop of a chaotic and lawless England during the Wars of the Roses.

With a dearth of central authority while the disputing royal families and foremost nobles fought it out for the throne, countryside matters were often resolved through brazen force and warfare, like when the Pastons' Caister Castle was seized by John Mowbray, 3rd Duke of Norfolk or when their Gresham manor house was stormed by Lord Moleyns while Margaret was inside.

What is even more remarkable, however, is Margaret's description of her detailed and dogged applications to have such property issues resolved by right and proper law, informing us of the grasp that educated people then had of the law. All this – and a wealth of fascinating household and lifestyle details – is revealed to us through a painstaking collection of letters that came to light over the years, culminating in the publication of a new and complete edition of the *Paston Letters* in 1904. This publication was an incredible six volumes long and contained 1,088 letters and papers.

◆

Cecily Neville, 1415–1495   *Duchess of York*

The great-granddaughter of John of Gaunt, mother of two monarchs and a queen-in-waiting in her own right as a duchess to Henry VI's designated heir, Richard Plantagenet, Duke of York, Cecily Neville was no dutiful cipher.

Called the 'Rose of Raby' (she was born at Raby Castle in County Durham) as the adored last child of Ralph Neville, 1st Earl of Westmoreland, her other nickname was 'Proud Cis' due to her pride, her temper and her headstrong nature. Probably more to do with the nature of the times, she managed to excite controversy at every turn.

When her son Edward (later King Edward IV) was born on a day that would have meant her husband was away for his conception, she ensured he was baptised hurriedly and without ceremony, provoking gossip in royal circles. This was later capitalised upon by Richard Neville, Earl of Warwick, when he fell out with Edward IV in 1469. It was he who spread the rumour that the king was a bastard and that his natural father was an archer named Benbourne of Rouen, where Cecily was based at the time.

Cecily was sensible enough to meet the whispers with silence, but when she wanted her son Richard to inherit the throne, much later in 1483, it was rumoured that she ruthlessly used the story to discredit the royal line of Edward – although this story is debated by historians today. This paved the way for the imprisonment and possible murder of his young sons in the Tower of London and the accession of Richard III.

When her husband and their second son Edmund were killed at the Yorkists' disastrous defeat at the battle of Wakefield in 1460, Cecily similarly rose above her grief and reacted swiftly, sending her youngest sons to the court of Philip III, the Duke of Burgundy, in a move that forced him to ally with the Yorkists.

Retreating to her childhood stronghold, now the headquarters and northern refuge for the Yorkists, Cecily was the power and cunning behind her sons' military successes. Once Edward IV was installed on the throne, she was an influential and proud parent and a nightmare mother-in-law to Edward's low-born wife, Elizabeth Woodville. After her dynastic machinations on her youngest son Richard's behalf ended in vain with his death at the Battle of Bosworth only two years after taking the throne, she bowed out of public life to head home and, in her last 10 years, earned herself a reputation for extreme piety – rather at odds with her earlier ruthless public image.

◆

Elizabeth Woodville, 1437–1492 *Queen to King Edward IV*

een in royal circles of the time as the equivalent of Edward IV marrying the girl-next-door, the marriage of the new king to his mistress Elizabeth Woodville outraged Edward's nearest and dearest, not least because, as it would later emerge, he had promised to marry another widow, Lady Eleanor Butler. Richard Neville – Earl of Warwick and 'Kingmaker' – had his own plans to marry Edward off, and was so furious at the news of the marriage that he abandoned his former protégé and changed sides to negotiate with Margaret of Anjou. But Elizabeth's Lancastrian connections and non-royal birth notwithstanding, Elizabeth was wily enough to seduce a lovestruck Edward IV into marrying her, and they went on to have 10 children together. Once installed as queen, she knitted a tight net of family around her, with some brazen social-climbing-style alliances – the most notorious of which was when she married her 20-year-old brother John Woodville off to the nearly 80-year-old Lady Katherine Neville.

As the favouritism became more blatant, she became more unpopular so, when Edward IV died suddenly in 1483, the Woodville clique was immediately cold-shouldered by the court. Elizabeth's children were declared illegitimate because of the Lady Eleanor Butler betrothal, and her two surviving sons – known to history as the Little Princes – were locked up in the Tower of London, where they met a mysterious and unexplained fate.

Elizabeth was forced to flee into sanctuary with her other children. Her gifts for matchmaking were called back into use, however, when Richard III assumed the throne. This time around, it was her daughter, Elizabeth – known as Elizabeth of York – who was sought as a badge of Yorkist legitimacy for Richard's claim to the throne.

Contemporaries were shocked by the rumour that Richard, after the death of his wife Anne, was angling to marry the young Elizabeth. However, before such plotting could come to fruition, the Battle of Bosworth intervened, resulting in the death of Richard III and Henry Tudor's ascent to the throne.

Seeking to cement his own claim to the throne, Henry VII married Elizabeth of York himself. Elizabeth Woodville was now a respectable queen mother but, not surprisingly, the king never quite trusted her, confiscating her estates and preferring for her to 'retire' to the nunnery of Bermondsey in 1487, where she died five years later.

CHAPTER X

◆

MERCENARIES & MILITARY MEN

Hugh d'Avranches, c. 1047–1101   *Military leader*

In the rough and ready days of the Norman Conquest, Hugh d'Avranches, Earl of Chester, fought so well for William I that he was granted a vast tranche of the Welsh Marches where he was ruler in all but name. Out there on the fringes of the conquest, such a 'kingdom' was not particularly easy to maintain. D'Avranches became famous for his relentless harrying of the Welsh and the brutal savagery of his military campaigns.

Years later, having survived the switches in power to William Rufus and Henry I, D'Avranches was becoming a caricature. One historian describes him as 'vicious, violent, addicted to gambling and sex; and so greedy that, weighed down by a mountain of fat, he could hardly move'. On the other hand, D'Avranches was not so easily pigeonholed as a simple brute. Not only was D'Avranches a friend and patron of Anselm of Canterbury, who became Archbishop of Canterbury, but he was also a generous giver to monasteries; he himself died a Benedictine monk. It was this mix of brutality and piety in fighting men such as D'Avranches that was to be the building blocks of the crusades in the centuries to come.

◆

William of Ypres, d. 1165   *Mercenary captain*

Having been expelled from his native Flanders in 1133, where he had overstepped himself and tried to live beyond the law, William of Ypres soon rose to become one of the leading mercenary captains in 'the Anarchy' in England. While he was King Stephen's most able and loyal commander, his skill led to the capture of Matilda's beloved half-brother, Robert of

Gloucester, and the Rout of Winchester in 1141, which proved an early turning point of the civil war. Ypres also gained notoriety for his violence and callousness. Blindness in middle age mellowed Ypres – he spent his money founding Boxley Abbey and his time in political mediation – most notably between King Stephen and Archbishop Theobald. By the time of his death, having retired to a monastery like Hugh d'Avranches before him, Ypres's violent, carpet-bagging past already seemed a lifetime away.

◆

William Marshal, 1147–1219   *'Greatest knight'*

The greatest jouster of the 12th century, William Marshal made his way through life on good looks, popular skills and his own wits. He managed to turn a career winning tournaments into a triumphant political rise that saw him undertake a successful crusade, serve five kings over nearly 50 years of public service, marry the second-richest heiress in England, have 10 healthy children and, in the sunset of his life, run the country as young Henry III's regent.

During his climb to power, he unhorsed the soon-to-be monarch, Richard I, but got away with it to the extent that Richard left him to guard his dominions in his absence. He also negotiated the successful signing of the Magna Carta between the barons and King John and was the subject of the first medieval biography to be written about a non-royal layman.

Marshal, however, was far from perfect. He was nicknamed *gaste-viande* ('guzzle-guts') for his appalling table manners, never bothered to read or write and, when on his estates in Ireland, reputedly indulged in his favourite pastime of beating up Irish peasants. All that said, however, Marshal still had a certain style and swagger that earned him both popularity among his contemporaries and a prominent place in history. By the end of his life, he had made his family one of the greatest in medieval England. He has been described as 'the greatest knight who ever lived'. Not bad for the younger son of a minor baron.

◆

Fawkes de Breauté, d. 1226   *Sheriff of Glamorgan*

Born the illegitimate son of a Norman knight, Fawkes de Breauté entered King John's service as a sergeant and departed it in disgrace. Along the way he became one of King John's most trusted henchmen, one of the leading royalist commanders in the civil unrest of 1215–1216 and a key player in the relief of Lincoln from French forces in 1217. For his military skills and prowess De Breauté was rewarded.

He was first appointed Sheriff of Glamorgan, and then given the guardianship of six important castles: Bedford, Buckingham, Cambridge, Hertford, Northampton and Oxford. He was also given the hand of the widowed Countess of Devon, but was never accepted by her relatives and neighbours as anything other than a thuggish, over-powerful, illiterate parvenu. By 1221 he was effectively drummed out of the West Country by the magnates of Devon and Cornwall.

That De Breauté was brutal is unquestionable – he burnt to death without trial a young man who had fallen in love with a Jewess and circumcised himself to convert to Judaism – but his greater crime was to overestimate his own social status. He forgot that the castles were not his at all, but the king's, and that the law would, ultimately, always be the victor. When

De Breauté refused to return 'his' castle at Bedford, he was summoned to court in 1224 to answer 35 charges, including the violent expulsion of freeholders from land that was not even his.

His brother William made the mistake of kidnapping one of the justices appointed to hear the case and took him to Bedford Castle, where they were besieged by the king's men. William was later hanged. De Breauté fled to Chester and onwards into exile, where he tried to plead his case with the pope, but died of food poisoning in 1226. Such was his unpopularity in England that Matthew Paris illustrated his passage on De Breauté's death with a picture of the devil ramming the suspect fish down De Breauté's gullet. As one historian concluded, 'self-made, he self-destructed'.

◆

Robert FitzWalter, 1170–1235   *Marshal of the Army of God*

As the self-styled Marshal of the Army of God, Robert FitzWalter managed to get away with leading the baronial opposition against King John, not just supporting it, but also actively inviting in the French invading force. He was captured at the Battle of Lincoln in 1217 and then released as part of the cautious amnesty agreed on Henry III's behalf by William Marshal. Thereafter he joined the establishment and actually appeared at the trial of Fawkes de Breauté alongside Hubert de Burgh, the king's man.

FitzWalter clearly had more guile than the average boxhead baron. His interests spanned the wine trade – he owned several vintners' ships – to the management of estates in the south of England and, through his wife, huge tracts of land in the north of England. When it came to King John, he managed to convert a personal grudge into a selfless crusade for human rights against a predatory monarch, to the extent that the pope made a kiss-and-make-up session between John and FitzWalter necessary as part of his 1213 deal to lift a Papal Interdict. But it didn't last. FitzWalter was the self-appointed leader of the pre- and post-Magna Carta baronial struggles with the monarch – cunningly managing to maintain a private army under the guise of running jousting tournaments – and was actually named as one of the 25 appointed to control royal actions. Not a bad result for one previously so uncontrollable himself. Even more surprising was his relative obscurity for the rest of his life. FitzWalter seems to have lived peacefully and within the law until he died in his bed in 1235.

◆

William Longsword, 1176–1226 and 1212–1250 *Father and son*

oth William Longsword the Elder and William Longsword the Younger were renowned for their loyalty and their bravery, making them as close to the ideals of chivalry as existed during that time; certainly more so than the more mercenary of fighters that came before or after them. Longsword the Elder was renowned for his courage both at sea and on the battlefield. For example, in 1213, he led a large fleet to Flanders where he routed the French flotilla; he also fought loyally for King John on the battlefields of Gascony and during the civil strife after the signing of the Magna Carta. He did, however, step out of line near the end of John's reign by appearing to fall in with a French invasion, but was rehabilitated during the minority of Henry III. He fought again in Gascony, but died soon after his return to England, reputedly poisoned by a jealous Hubert de Burgh.

A bizarre footnote to Longsword the Elder's life was that, for some reason or other, his tomb was opened in 1691, and the well-preserved corpse of a rat was found inside his skull.

Longsword the Younger spent much of his life overseas, earning glorious accolades for his conduct on the battlefields of the Holy Land. When mismanagement by the commanders of the Seventh Crusade led the allied armies into a hopeless situation at the Battle of Mansor, the bungling Count Robert of Artois shouted at Longsword to flee. Longsword hardly stopped fighting to shout back: 'God forbid that a son of my father should flee any Saracen, I would rather die happily than live unhappily.' The story then goes that, even when surrounded by a vastly superior infidel army, Longsword the Younger fought on 'when the feet were cut off his exhausted horse, but he still severed the heads, hands and feet of his assailants'. Even when his own hand was cut off, he fought on left-handed; finally perishing from countless wounds, with his faithful men throwing themselves over his body to protect him from mutilation. It was the work of legend.

◆

Sir John Chandos, d. 1370 *Founding father of the Order of the Garter*

A close friend of Edward the Black Prince and a founding member of the Order of the Garter, Sir John Chandos was described by contemporaries as 'the bravest of the brave'. As such, he was closer to Chaucer's 'very gentil, parfait knight' than many others contained within these pages, yet he was of humble birth. He only happened to come to royal notice when, as a veteran of the French wars, he led the 16-year-old

Prince Edward's troops to victory at the battle of Crécy and then provided the military brains behind the strategy that won the battle of Poitiers. Being of non-noble birth, he might have inspired jealousy from less-favoured peers, but chroniclers are unanimous in noting his popularity. 'There was none more beloved and esteemed than he was among the knights and leaders of his time,' said one. He was also very much in demand. When the Black Prince wanted him to help govern Aquitaine from 1362, Chandos was tempted away by John Montfort, Duke of Brittany, who needed his skills on the battlefield against his rival, Charles du Bois.

Chandos never forgot where he came from. In 1368, he opposed Edward's plans to impose the common-man-crippling hearth tax in Gascony to pay for more war, lobbied for peace between England and France and retired, on principle, to the estates in Normandy that had been his reward. However, Edward was forced to eat humble pie a year later when he begged Chandos to come back to repulse a sudden French counter-attack. When Chandos was killed in an unnecessary skirmish on New Year's Eve, he was mourned as an honourable man by French and English, humble bowman and baron alike.

◆

Sir John Hawkwood, 1320–1394 *Mercenary fighter*

To some, he was the quintessence of the glorious fighting ideal; to others, Sir John Hawkwood was a hired thug who couldn't even read his own mercenary contracts. In any case he became such a prominent success as a mercenary that he helped promote the image of the tough English knight throughout Europe. Supposedly the second son of a mere tanner, Hawkwood rose through the ranks of the English Army in the first stages of the Hundred Years' War, probably fighting at Crécy and at Poitiers.

He had left the English army by 1360, and rose to the command of the White Company, which soon gained itself a reputation for military skill and ruthlessness. It was Hawkwood's skills on the battlefield, and in playing his employers and their enemies off against each other, that earned him the nickname *l'acuto* ('the sharp one'). In his 31 years of being a mercenary in Italy, Hawkwood acquired estates in the Romagna, castles in Tuscany, the hand of the Duke of Milan's (illegitimate) daughter and a patina of respectability that allowed Richard II to appoint him an ambassador to the Roman court in 1381. For the last few years of his life, having defended Florence against the Milanese, Hawkwood was given citizenship and a pension by the grateful city. He was buried in the city's cathedral in 1394, although the king asked for his body to be sent back to England.

Some 50 years later, Hawkwood's name was still a byword for self-made brilliance. Around the mid-1430s one chronicler noted how 'a large contingent of master craftsmen and apprentices, in their spare hours, read the chap-book lives of Sir John Hawkwood and Sir Richard Whittington and aspire to marry their master's daughter and become Lord Mayor'.

◆

Sir John Fastolf, 1378–1459 *Military man*

o some extent the model for William Shakespeare's rogue knight Falstaff and the classic example of a war profiteer of the medieval age, Sir John Fastolf had earned his stripes in the latter stages of the Hundred Years' War, serving on the French front until 1440, when he was over 60 years of age. He was clearly a military man of some ingenuity – at what was to become known as the Battle of the Herrings, he successfully defended a supply train ambushed by the French by barricading in his men with barrels of herrings. However, he was unfairly accused of cowardice at the retreat from Patay, temporarily stripped of his Order of the Garter and, although later cleared and reinstated, suffered from a bad reputation thereafter.

What Fastolf was truly skilled at, however, was the husbandry of war – making money not just from the rewards and honours given to him, but also from the hiring-out of troops and other slightly sharp endeavours.

After amassing his wealth, Fastolf retired home to Norfolk where he featured prominently in the *Paston Letters* as an irascible, greedy old man, still ruthless to the point of brutality in his business dealings, 'for the most part without pity and mercy'. As a patron of the arts during his life, childless Fastolf had intended to bequeath his great wealth to the Church, but ended up leaving most of it to his neighbours and friends, the Pastons.

◆

ON THE EDGE: MYSTICS, MARTYRS, WITCHES & HERETICS

Wulfric of Haselbury, 1090–1155   *Anchorite and prophet*

Having started life as a priest more interested in hunting than in working in his ministry, it was quite a U-turn for Wulfric of Haselbury when, after a chance conversation with an itinerant beggar, he chose to take the ascetic path. He settled in as an anchorite in a permanently enclosed cell 20 miles from Exeter in Devon, in the village of Haselbury Plucknett where he was supported by the Cluniac monks of Montacute, who brought him food and cared for him. He became renowned for his penance-driven regime, with its prostrate fasts and constant long immersions in cold water.

Haselbury's apparent gift for prophecy and second sight began to gather important visitors: between 1129 and 1133, when Stephen of Blois was still 'merely' a count, he stopped off to visit Haselbury's cell. Stephen was startled to be addressed as king by Haselbury and returned, as king, in 1142, presumably hoping for more good news. Haselbury instead lectured King Stephen on his misgovernment of England and referred to a mysterious sin for which he must do penance before he could hold the throne peacefully. Haselbury died in 1155. Gradually, his tomb began to acquire a reputation as a holy site. Innumerable miracles were said to have taken place there from 1185–1235, making the village of Haselbury a popular pilgrimage destination.

◆

Christina of Markyate, 1097–1161   *Benedictine nun*

Rather than marry the local nobleman to whom her parents had betrothed her, Christina of Markyate ran away from home, committed herself to a life of celibacy and lived in hiding with a local hermit for four years. She spent the time fasting, meditating and experiencing visions while sheltering in a particularly small cell. Her family and betrothed finally released her from her obligations in 1122, leaving her to found a Benedictine nunnery at Markyate in Hertfordshire, under the patronage of the monastery at St Albans, where she spent the rest of her life.

It was Markyate's ability to nurture friendships with her male 'colleagues' that ensured that her piety and that of her female followers could proceed undisturbed. A skilful needlewoman, she sent Pope Adrian IV off to Rome with an embroidered mitre and sandals. The monks at St Albans created the famous *St Albans Psalter* especially for her, a masterpiece containing the 'Legend of Alexis' about a religious leader who left his wife on their wedding night to pursue a life of devotion and willing asceticism.

◆

Nun of Watton, c. mid-12th century — *Rebellious nun*

Religious extremism hit new lows with the case of the Nun of Watton, who had been admitted to the Gilbertine convent of Watton as a toddler. According to legend she was a rebellious teenager who seduced a lay brother at the neighbouring monastery and then fell pregnant. Outraged, the nuns argued over whether to burn her, roast her or skin her alive, but first decided to use her to lure the lay brother into a trap. The Nun of Watton evaded her fate by castrating her lover with her own hands. Afterwards, she was 'miraculously deprived of her pregnancy' and retired to a life of blameless celibacy in the convent.

Roland le Pettour, c. mid to late 12th century   *Court jester*

Not quite a mystic, martyr or heretic, but definitely operating on the edge of what we would now consider to be polite society was Roland le Pettour, or Roland the Farter, a jester in the service of Henry II. Even when retired, Le Pettour performed once a year in front of his master, 'one jump, one whistle and one fart' – 'unum saltum, unum sifflettum et unum bumbulum'. He was richly criticised for this by the clerics of the court, including the chronicler Peter of Blois, with the line from Psalm 14: 'The fool says in his heart, There is no God!' But the last laugh went to Le Pettour. He was richly rewarded, being given 30 acres of land in Suffolk. Not a bad wage for a bit of hot air once a year.

◆

Dame Alice Kyteler, b. 1289   *Ireland's last witch*

A story well-known in England in the 14th century, and often invoked by people wanting to issue a warning against witchcraft, was that of Dame Alice Kyteler. She was Ireland's last witch who, having supposedly poisoned all four of her husbands, was then accused in 1325 of their murders by her sons from the various marriages. Certainly the evidence was colourful and incriminating.

Her husbands were said to have each become 'emaciated, nails dropped off and with no hair on their bodies' before they died; and at her house, her sons just happened to find a sacrificial wafer with the devil's name on it and a broomstick on which, they said, she was known to 'amble and gallop' through the town of Kilkenny. The fact that she had a prosperous moneylending business, inherited from her own father, which she intended to pass only to her favourite son, William, was presumably nothing to do with the actions of her other jealous sons...

In the end, Kyteler's maid, Petronella, was burnt as a witch, her son William got away with a penance that paid for the re-roofing of St Canice's Cathedral and her other sons got their hands on her business. As for Kyteler, she disappeared, apparently escaping to England. Nothing more was heard of her.

◆

Richard Rolle, 1300–1349   *Hermit and mystic*

Yorkshireman Richard Rolle was the first of the great English mystics. He was a strongly emotional theologian, Bible translator and dedicated hermit who interspersed years of solitude with years of wandering before finally settling at the Cistercian priory of Hampole near Doncaster, where he died in 1349. He said his mystical experiences were like a roaring flame burning inside him, accompanied by sweet spiritual singing. This he used as an excuse to stay away from conventional church services, claiming that he could no longer bear to hear the discordances of mortal singing!

Regarded as a saint during his life and with a tomb celebrated for its miraculous properties, Rolle was never canonized. However, he was hugely influential in the amount of scripture he translated into English, opening up the mysteries of Church teachings long before John Wycliffe was lauded (and prosecuted) for doing the same.

Many of his works were destroyed in his lifetime as too radical for the times. Luckily, the good nuns of Hampole, who had nursed Rolle in his final years, had kept untampered-with copies of his works in their library.

John of Nottingham, d. 1325 *Necromancer*

In 1324, under the tyrannous yoke of the Despensers and a dominated Edward II, thuggery was rampant, with 27 defendants being tried for plotting against Edward II and his favoured, but popularly hated courtiers. A number of wealthy citizens of Coventry hired a necromancer – a magician of the dark arts – to kill the king, the Despensers and the king's courtiers.

Modelling wax dolls to represent the targets, John of Nottingham and his servant Robert Marshall decided to test one before proceeding. They chose a courtier named Richard de Sowe. First they stuck hot pins through the doll and then slowly melted it before a fire. News came next morning that De Sowe had been suffering terrible pains and a high fever that night, so Nottingham took a pin and plunged it through the heart of what remained of the wax image. This was all too much for Marshall.

When it emerged that De Sowe had indeed died, Marshall fled to the authorities and confessed their crime. All the conspirators were arrested but Nottingham died in prison before the trial. Interestingly, the 27 good burghers of Coventry were all acquitted – as real an indication as any that even the authorities could understand why they had been so desperate as to dabble in the dark arts in the first place.

◆

John Wycliffe, c. 1330–1384 *Father of Lollardy*

Revered as the intellectual inspiration behind the Lollards (England's first significant movement railing against the orthodox Church), it is surprising to note that Yorkshireman John Wycliffe was, in fact, an armchair champion who rarely preached publicly. He devoted his entire life to reform within Catholicism through academic writings and Church politics. Starting with the supremacy of scripture (he was the first to advocate a full translation of the Bible into English, a wish his pupils then followed up), he soon began to argue against the orthodoxy of the Roman Catholic establishment, to question papal authority and to reject monasticism and the so-called 'contemplative' life. Heretically, he also argued against the 'real presence' of God during the ceremony of the Eucharist – the transubstantiation of the bread for the body – and the wine for the blood, of Christ.

Unlike his later followers, however, Wycliffe enjoyed the support of the enormously powerful John of Gaunt and Joan, Princess of Wales, and his advocacy of civil control over ecclesiastical excesses found a measure of acceptance at court.

'Every second man that you meet is a Lollard,' wrote one admiring contemporary. This was the honeymoon period of Lollardy. Thereafter, the Peasants' Revolt of 1381, the increasing radicalism of the Lollards and the dissemination of ideas outside the hallowed halls of Oxford into the less controllable levels of secular society began to alienate the political elite as well as the religious leaders. Oldcastle's Rebellion of 1414 forever associated Lollardy with public disorder and the Lollard movement began to fragment, going underground as the persecution became more draconian. Ultimately, this could be said to have ensured its survival, its lack of leader or formal structure making it impossible to stamp out. The fact that prosecutions were still going on at a county level well into the 16th century testifies to its continuing grass-roots appeal, passing down within families' generations eventually to be absorbed into Lutheranism and Protestantism. In 1427 Wycliffe's remains were exhumed, burned and the ashes cast into the River Swift. This was a vain attempt by the establishment to wash him out of the consciousness of the English.

Julian of Norwich, 1342–c. 1413   *Mystic and visionary*

Julian of Norwich was a renowned anchoress, mystic and visionary whose wisdom and theological insight would be thought of as cutting-edge even today. With *The Revelations of Divine Love* (c. 1393), Julian produced probably the first book written by a woman in the English language and one of the most individually famous lines of Catholic theology 'all shall be well, and all shall be well, and all manner of thing shall be well' – despite the plague-ridden turmoil of her times. Her optimism was all the more remarkable given the hardship of her life – voluntarily locked into a cell with only an open slot for food deliveries and the constant stream of visitors that came to her for advice and pastoral guidance.

It all started in 1373 when she was 30, severely ill and undergoing a near-death experience in the form of an intense series of visions. She became a renowned spiritual authority. In the complicated, unstable years of the 14th century, her simple 'hazlenut' theory – that God made even the tiniest of things because he loves us – must have been a welcome change from the usual 'fire and brimstone' teachings of her day which put forward the idea that the sufferings of poverty and the plague were divine punishment.

◆

Margery Kempe, 1373– c. 1438   *Autobiographer and religious convert*

It's hard to know where to start when listing the remarkable – and often contradictory – things that have been written about Margery Kempe. She has provided us with the earliest surviving autobiography ever to be written in English, yet she could not read or write herself. For 40 years, she had long conversations with Christ while weeping and wailing her way around the various pilgrimage sites of Europe and Asia. But was she a genuine mystic or merely an hysteric, unbalanced by a post-natal nervous breakdown after her first child was born? She had no less than 13 more children despite throwing herself out of the window and attempting to 'bite through the veins in her wrist' after the birth of her first.

She was an ambitious businesswoman in her hometown of King's Lynn (then just Bishop's Lynn), delighting in clothes, jewellery and all the trappings of prosperity, yet spent most of her life begging the church authorities to allow her just to wear a plain white dress as a sign of her piety and simplicity. Especially bizarre, given the cloistered age in which she lived in, was the ambivalent relationship she had with her own sexuality. Her autobiography explains that she oscillated between rampant lustiness and extreme chastity, so that on one occasion, while desperate to stick to her vow of celibacy (even within her marriage) she found herself propositioning a young stranger outside her church.

Further visions of Jesus led to life commitment to God and an intrepid journey around the pilgrimage hotspots of Jerusalem, Rome, Santiago de Compostela, and even Danzig. This was interspersed by fireside debates with leading priests of the day and regular imprisonment, and occasional death threats, for preaching in public, which was forbidden for laypersons, let alone women. All the while, she exercised long and loudly her 'gift of weeping' and fasting, before finally settling down to dictate her life story to two carefully supervised scribes.

Perhaps the most surprising thing about Kempe is that, for all the drama, colour and hysterical contradiction of her life, *The Book of Margery Kempe* (c. 1435) is, by contrast, not only a carefully structured spiritual and social commentary – with a sharpness towards both Church and state institutions and corruptions – but a fascinating insight into the life of a middle-class medieval woman.

Eleanor Cobham, c. 1400–1452 *Aristocrat and 'witch'*

espite being an English aristocrat when she married Humphrey, Duke of Gloucester (younger brother of Henry V and regent uncle of Henry VI), Eleanor Cobham's elevated position didn't stop her from conspiring to kill her nephew-in-law. However, what brought Cobham lasting notoriety was that her method of murder was deemed to be witchcraft and she was accused of both treason and sorcery.

Together with her chaplain Roger Bolingbroke and two other priests, she was said to have melted a wax figure under a gentle heat, hoping that as it melted away, the king's own strength would unsuspiciously melt away and he would die, leaving her husband as heir to the throne. The most Cobham would admit to was having asked Bolingbroke – who was said to deal in the dark arts – just to calculate how long the king would live. The three priests were executed but Cobham was spared, although she was made to walk three times through the city bearing a lighted taper and then imprisoned on the Isle of Man for 14 years until her death. Peel Castle, her prison there, is still said to be haunted by her ghost. Apparently there wasn't a day when she didn't attempt either to escape or to kill herself.

CHAPTER XII

◆

GOOD WITH THEIR HANDS:
ARTISTS & CRAFTSMEN

Ailnoth Ingeniator, c. 1140–1197 *Engineer*

Ailnoth 'The Engineer' might sound a little Quentin Tarantino-esque to us today, but Ailnoth Ingeniator's ingenuity had a little more substance than this would suggest. To be an engineer (or ingeniator) in the 12th century had very little to do with the oil-stained or number-crunching realities of today's post-industrialism; rather, it meant the practical ability to invent devices, usually battlefield weapons, like the great war 'engines', slings and siege machines. Ingeniator himself came through the ranks of the army to work for Henry II on the Tower of London and Westminster Palace and was admired by contemporaries as a versatile craftsman, able to work as easily with glass or metal as with stone or wood. From the ructions of 'the Anarchy' through to the Great Rebellion by the king's sons in 1173–1174 and the rumblings thereafter, the skills to build, maintain, adapt and, in the case of rebellious nobles such as the Earl of Norfolk's castle, tear down all manner of buildings was the secret of Ingeniator's success.

◆

Matthew Paris, c. 1200–1259 *Chronicler and illustrator*

In 1255, Louis IX gave Henry III the first elephant to be seen on English shores. Matthew Paris, the most famous of medieval chroniclers, drew it from life for his *Chronica Majora* (*Greater Chronicle*, c. 1259), producing the first accurate drawing of an elephant at that time; previously, elephants had been depicted like a type of wild boar with an extended snout. Paris proved to be a talented illustrator to whom we owe much of our visual sense of the age.

Having joined the rich and well-connected monastery of St Albans in 1217, Paris was based there for the rest of his life, constantly in touch with barons, kings and all the highest echelons of society in the Middle Ages, both secular and ecclesiastical. When, in 1257, Henry III spent a week at St Albans, the king kept Paris beside him at all times and, as he said, 'guided my pen with much good will and diligence'; Paris also acted as an ambassador for Louis IX to Scandinavia.

Described as 'courtier and scholar, monk and man of the world', Paris's greatest work, the *Chronica Majora* recounts England's history from the Creation to 1259. His clear narrative, vivid anecdotes and telling epigrams are all rendered in eloquently employed Latin. Vivid word-pictures like Paris's view of the pope's emissaries as 'harpies and bloodsuckers, plunderers, who not merely shear, but skin, the sheep' are complemented by simple – almost cartoon-strip-style – drawings that bring the narrative leaping off the page. Paris was centuries ahead of his time in trying to involve multiple senses when approaching his work. The first seven pages of the *Chronica Majora* are a visual and tactile feast, a kind of medieval road map – complete with interactive flaps and fold-outs – that leads the reader along a journey from London to Jerusalem.

◆

Henry de Reyns, d. 1253   *Architect*

igh up on the first level of Westminster Abbey's interior is the carved head of a stonemason in the thoughtful pose meant to denote the higher status of designer or architect. It is supposedly a homage to Henry de Reyns, the man responsible for putting Westminster Abbey on the map.

As part of his great interest in Edward the Confessor, Henry III wanted to continue the work that his far-off predecessor had started: the building of Westminster Abbey. He had most of the existing church dismantled and sent off to his leading architect, De Reyns, to study French cathedrals and the Gothic style. De Reyns soon surpassed his brief with a speedy and efficient building programme from 1245–1269, which included a lavish shrine to the Confessor, a throne, a Coronation Theatre and delicate Gothic vaulting of the nave that, at over 100 feet high, made it the highest in England. De Reyns died in 1253; Henry III died in 1272, with the Abbey virtually complete. But with its two Henrys now gone, the heart and soul of the enterprise had been ripped out. Westminster Abbey wasn't finished until 1745 to the design of one of England's most famous architects, Christopher Wren.

◆

W de Wycombe, mid to late 13th century *Composer*

Possibly the oldest example of a counterpoint (singing in a round, as in 'London Bridge is Falling Down') in existence is 'Sumer is Icumen In'. It is also the most famous tune of the Middle Ages – before Henry VIII's 'Greensleeves'. It is thought to have been composed in 1260, but achieved its highest level of notoriety when it was used in the cult 1973 film, *The Wicker Man*, starring Christopher Lee and Edward Woodward. The composer of 'Sumer is Icumen In' was thought to have been the enigmatically signed 'W de Wycombe' who composed from the rural obscurity of Herefordshire. His most productive decades were the 1270s and 1280s, when he attracted renown for his polyphonic alleluias. Today, we only have one complete rendition of such pieces, with nearly 60 other manuscripts revealing only fragments.

Henry Yevele, c. 1320–1400   *Architect*

Henry Yevele was the most productive and, some say, the greatest architect/mason in late medieval England. He is often considered the 14th century's Christopher Wren: both survived the scourge of plague to leave their mark in brick, mortar and stone across several counties' skylines. He was as industrious in secular monuments as he was in ecclesiastical ones, and also managed to earn a good living as one of the two wardens of London Bridge.

Chapels, churches and cloisters went hand-in-hand with more worldly commissions: John of Gaunt's Savoy Palace, London's Charterhouse, the Jewel Tower and the Great Hall of the Palace of Westminster. Castles across the south of England were his bread and butter; nobles' tombs – such as Edward III's own monument – were the jam. He even foreshadowed the work of IKEA by 600 years when he designed and carved the great Neville screen of Caen stone for the altar of Durham Cathedral from 1372–1380, then shipped it up there in boxes.

◆

Geoffrey Chaucer, c. 1340–1400   *Poet*

Even though, at 17,000 words, it is unfinished, *The Canterbury Tales* (c. 1390) is hailed by many as one of the most brilliant works in all English literature, and certainly the best piece of creative writing to have come out of the medieval era. Its author, Geoffrey Chaucer, seems to have been a polymath, a man who combined a successful career as a civil servant with a huge energy for writing in his spare time – the first great poet to write in English – and a courtier who rose above early rumours of rape.

Born to a respectable London wine merchant, Chaucer was better connected at court than most of his contemporaries. He was the controller of the London customs on furs, skins and hides from 1374–1386, a JP and an MP in 1385–1386 and clerk of the works from 1389. These positions supplemented his modest inheritance and left him otherwise free to read and write, both of which he did voraciously, in English, French, Latin and Italian.

Chaucer read anything and everything, from bawdy romances to the latest philosophical treatises and fed these wide-ranging ingredients into his many publications, culminating in the multi-coloured tapestry of chivalry, ribaldry, history and satire that is *The Canterbury Tales*. Even the structure of the work was revolutionary. His technique of introducing his stories through the mouths of pilgrims on their way to the shrine of Thomas Becket brought the traditional bard method of storytelling vividly alive and offered a wealth of insights into the life and times of the poet himself.

Chaucer's greatness was nearly obscured by the Great Vowel Shift of 1400 (the year of his death), which suddenly made both the metre and vocabulary of his work more difficult to convey. However, by the 16th century, his legacy was universally acknowledged. John Dryden praised him as 'the father of English poetry' and Edmund Spenser deemed him 'the well of English undefiled'.

◆

William Wynford, c. 1340–1405 *Architect*

William Wynford, master mason from 1365 and the great architect who gave us the exquisite nave of Winchester Cathedral, was well connected enough to be picked up quickly by William Wykeham and was thereafter well placed in the royal patronage of the 14th century. He was one of the first architects who can be said to have had a personal style and a keen eye can spot the Wynford touch in a variety of churches both mighty and humble. He restyled Winchester Cathedral into one of the masterpieces of the English Perpendicular Gothic school, worked on elements of Windsor Castle, New College Oxford, Wardour Castle and Yeovil Church and, most famously, came up with an ingenious solution for Wells Cathedral's heavy and sinking crossing tower. Known as 'scissor arches', he used inverted 'strainer' arches to brace and stabilise the piers of the crossing from the inside, providing a cheaper and quicker solution to rebuilding. He had the unusual satisfaction of being able to see the completion of his work (unlike most cathedral-builders), although he died soon after.

◆

John Dunstable, c. 1380–1453 *Composer*

Despite being the greatest English composer of the Middle Ages (before William Byrd knocked him off his perch), we know little about John Dunstable except for the bald facts that he was born in Kent, lived in France, probably visited Italy and died on Christmas Eve in 1453, all the while serving the Duke of Bedford. The paucity of biographical information is all the more frustrating given his widespread fame across Europe.

Fifty-five of his surviving works have cropped up all over the Continent and it is repeatedly documented that his *contenance anglaise* (English touch) influenced music in a number of countries for over a century. His approach was characterised by a fresher vocal line, an increased depth of tone or sonority and a more pronounced feeling for the richness of chords.

As a French poet wrote: 'The English guise they wear with grace/They follow Dunstable aright/And thereby have they learned apace/To make their music gay and bright.'

◆

Blind Harry, c. 1440–1492   *Minstrel*

Blind Harry the Minstrel, although he concerned himself mainly with Scottish events, is the most famous example of a trade that flourished throughout the Middle Ages – the trade of the minstrel, the troubadour, the bard, the travelling storyteller. Meaning, literally, 'little servant', minstrels were at first just servants at court who occasionally entertained courtiers and barons with *chansons de geste* or their local equivalent, but later minstrels were dedicated performers, paid to entertain their lords with music and song.

Blind Harry was most likely of noble Scottish birth and it is believed that he was either sightless from birth or was blinded during military service. He is best-known for his epic, 12-volume work on Scottish freedom fighter William 'Braveheart' Wallace, written 170 years after Wallace's death. In it Wallace assumes various disguises and travels freely around Europe dressed as a monk, an old woman and a potter. While enlisting support for the Scottish cause in France, Blind Harry tells how Wallace first defeated two reigning champions in a French tournament, then a lion, before asking the king of France: 'Are there any more dogs you would have slain?'

Blind Harry's adoration of Wallace was not just for the love of a hero; patriotism and nationalism had as much to do with it. As a paid courtier of James IV of Scotland, even a minstrel was involved in the medieval equivalent of spin-doctoring.